Ray Laenen

Joe Mazzara

LIBERTY SHIP SURVIVOR

Why Ray Laenen is so Proud to be an American

by
Joseph N. Mazzara

authorHOUSE™

1663 LIBERTY DRIVE, SUITE 200
BLOOMINGTON, INDIANA 47403
(800) 839-8640
WWW.AUTHORHOUSE.COM

First published by AuthorHouse 03/24/05

ISBN: 1-4208-4124-6 (sc)
ISBN: 1-4208-4160-2 (dj)

Library of Congress Control Number: 2005902389

Printed in the United States of America
Bloomington, Indiana

This book is printed on acid-free paper.

Cover design by Bryan Thompson.

All photos courtesy of Ray Laenen Private Collection unless otherwise noted.

For the children of Ray and Norma Laenen -
Gary, Rick, Carrie, Bob, Kim and their families.

Table of Contents

Preface

At Christmastime 2003, my sister-in-law, Andrea Van Slembrouck, approached me with an idea. Andrea's good friend Carrie Pleva had casually mentioned that her father was interested in having someone write up his story. Andrea didn't know the details of the story, but she knew that Ray Laenen had been "lost at sea" during World War II. Being a writer and an aficionado of WWII history, I was, naturally, interested in meeting him. Andrea gave me his phone number and I called him to arrange our first meeting. At this point, I was not sure that there would be enough material here for a magazine article, let alone a book.

I met Ray and Norma Laenen on one of the coldest days of January 2004. I brought my wife along to help break the ice (not literally), as Cindy's family had known the Laenens for many years. They lived less than a mile from each other and both families were longtime parishioners at nearby St. Gertrude Catholic Church.

Bundled up in down jackets and heavy boots, Cindy and I were welcomed into the Laenen home and made to feel as if we were the two most important visitors the Laenens had ever received. I soon found that this feeling was shared by virtually all who know this family.

We stayed for three hours that first day, while Ray told us his tale. He showed us a video of a presentation he had made for the Library of Congress Veteran's History Project, and many old photographs of his war days. But it was in his own emotional retelling of this defining moment of his life, that I began to see that there was a lot more here than a mere story of survival at sea. This is also the story of a Belgian immigrant who, at the age of 79, still beams with pride at the fact that he is an American Citizen and patriot. This is the story of an eternal optimist, a man who's faith in God and in himself were never shaken - even as he floated for twenty-two days in a crowded lifeboat in the Indian Ocean. This is the story of a man who, fifty years after the sinking of his Liberty Ship, went to Germany to meet and forgive some of the men who were responsible for his near-death experience.

Tears welled up in Ray Laenen's eyes as he told of the events of almost sixty years before. With the intensity of a Baptist preacher, he punctuated his story with arm gestures, vocal modulation and, where necessary, passionate pauses for effect. His still-athletic body and ruggedly handsome looks belied his age, as he once more relived the defining moment of his life. Throughout the afternoon, I was struck with two things. First, Ray Laenen is an exemplar of what Tom Brokaw has called the Greatest Generation. He served with honor in the war and asks for no thanks other than the remembrance that freedom is not free. Second, Ray Laenen's faith is so strong that he allows very little room for the possibility of coincidence. So many times in his life things have happened that seem to defy the probabilities of chance. Each sign, in Ray's eyes, was another marker to confirm that he was on the right road.

At the end of our first meeting I told Ray that he clearly had enough here to fill the pages of a book. Over the next year, I met with him many times to glean the details of his story. As the book took shape, we would invariably find just one more anecdote to include and just one more person to contact or add to the story.

I have many people to thank for their assistance, not the least of whom are Ray and Norma Laenen. In addition to his incredible memory for details, Ray also had an immense collection of photographs that made my job so much easier. In fact, I had some trouble deciding which photos to leave out of the book, as there were far too many to use. Also, I thank Carrie Pleva and Andrea Van Slembrouck for bringing Ray and me together so that this story could be told.

As with any project of this nature there are many others to thank: Ken Laabs for his first hand account of mule skinning along the Burma Road; Tom Tschirhart, Tom Spicketts, Don Tuthill and Chuck Kemmer for their personal recollections of Ray Laenen the person, and of the sinking of the *SS Peter Silvester*. Roman Godzek of the Archdiocese of Detroit and Donna Westley of the Sisters of the Immaculate Heart of Mary for their assistance in providing photographs of the old St. Rose of Lima church and school buildings; Bryan Thompson for his riveting cover design; Neal Shine for being the spiritual godfather of all Detroit area writers, and for being kind enough to review my manuscript prior to publication; finally, thanks as always to my wife Cindy, and to my children Kate and Mark for their proofreading and editing assistance.

It is my hope that readers of this book will be as enthralled as I was with Ray Laenen's fascinating story, and will never forget that freedom is not free.

Joe Mazzara
February, 2005

Chapter One

A Belgian Family Comes to America

All of our people all over the country - except the pure blooded Indians – are immigrants or descendents of immigrants, including even those who came over here on the Mayflower.
– Franklin D. Roosevelt

Amerca is not so much a great melting pot as it is a sturdy rope, which derives its strength from the winding of its many different strands. Generations of immigrants have come to American shores, to continually replenish those strands. In so doing, each new person has brought with him or her a special quality that, when added to the rope, further strengthens the whole. Still, it is upon the close examination of a single life that we come to understand the source of that diverse strength. This is the story of one of those strands. The story of the making of an American patriot.

Remie "Ray" Laenen added his strand to the fabric of America in 1927. His parents left their Belgian homeland in search of freedom and opportunity in the United States. They found both, but not before their firstborn son would learn the profound truth that freedom has its cost. Remie Laenen's life has, in many ways, exemplified the long (and, nowadays, often maligned) tradition of the American Patriot. He came to the shores of America from a foreign land, and would later defend our freedom as a soldier on an iconic American Liberty Ship. Three rounds of torpedoes from a German U-boat would sink Ray Laenen's ship, but not his spirit, nor his unwavering sense of patriotism. Twenty-two days adrift in a lifeboat in the Indian Ocean only served to strengthen his resolve and pride to be an American.

The American spirit took such deep roots in this Belgian immigrant, that he not only prospered in his new country, but also eventually traveled to Germany to meet and forgive the very men who sank his ship! Today, he spends his free time talking with the children of modern America, to remind them of the lesson he learned – that freedom is not free.

Remie Laenen was born in April 1926, in the small Flemish farming village of Oevel, twenty-five miles east of Antwerp, Belgium. He was named after his grandfather who was, as were most men in that community, a farmer. The few who were not farmers typically worked as diamond cutters in nearby Antwerp. Remie's father, Gustaf, however, had bigger ideas. While it would have been quite natural for Gustaf to continue in the farming life of his father, he had other dreams. This, for Gustaf, was a time of opportunity and ambition. He wanted to find out for himself what the world was like outside of Oevel.

In 1921, Gustaf Laenen was twenty-seven years old and the First World War had ended just three years earlier. In that *War To End*

All Wars (!), the Germans had (as had many other armies) occupied Belgium. With the World War over, Belgium was now enjoying a period of peace and freedom which was well appreciated by a people who had endured a long history of war and occupation by outside forces. Last time it had been the Germans, but before that seemingly everyone from the Romans to the Spaniards, Charlemagne and Napoleon Bonaparte had at one time or another trod uninvited across Belgian soil. In fact, Napoleon's defeat at Waterloo occurred just a few miles south of Brussels.

It is not that the Belgians were war-like people, they were not; or even that they had a stake in most of the battles that were waged on their land. It was simply that by geographic happenstance, they were strategically located in the middle of Europe, between the North Sea and the perceived targets of a multitude of conquerors. Unknown to Gustaf Laenen and the other inhabitants of Belgium in peaceful 1921, there would be another major conflict fought on their soil by foreign nations within the next twenty years. This one would involve the Laenen family directly.

Gustaf Laenen enjoyed the new peace, but did not want to spend the rest of his life in Oevel. He knew where he wanted to go. Many Belgians had emigrated from Belgium to America in the years just after the First World War. With the war finally over in Belgium, much of the countryside and many of the villages had been destroyed, and there were not many jobs for the returning soldiers.

Gustaf had read enough about America to know that it was a place of promise and opportunity, yet he was torn. He was the oldest of seventeen children. At twenty seven, the only job he had ever held was to help out his family at home and on the farm. Gustaf, like most firstborn sons in such a family, was raised to have a strong sense of responsibility for the others. If he were to leave, he would

3

feel that he was abandoning that responsibility to the family. Still, he did not want to grow old in Oevel, especially as a farmer or a diamond cutter.

Gustaf Laenen (second from left in back) and his family in Belgium

Ultimately, ambition won out over familial responsibility, and Gustaf went to America. While no other family members went with him, he did not go alone. At that time, one could not immigrate to America without first having a "sponsor" who would vouch for you, find you a job, and hopefully, a place to live. Gustaf knew that three of the Van Doninck brothers from the nearby city of Geel were planning to move to America. They agreed to take Gustaf with them. One of the brothers had arranged for work as a baker in Gresham, Oregon, so Gustaf left his family behind, and learned the baking trade in America.

Still a bachelor, Gustaf stayed in Oregon for three years. In 1924, partly out of loneliness and partly from an overwhelming sense of responsibility for his family, he returned to Belgium. Living without family in a new country had made him feel homesick. A Belgian writer would, many years later, sum up the feelings of Detroit's transplanted Belgians. In the penultimate paragraph of his 1983 book entitled *150 Years of Flemings in Detroit*, Arthur Verthe writes:

> *"In the museums of Detroit there are works of great Flemish masters. In the hearts of thousands of Flemish Americans lives the love for that small patch of land on the North Sea and for its song that echoes in the palms of their extended hands."* (Verthe, pg. 124).

Gustaf's decision to return to Belgium turned out to be fortuitous. Shortly after his return to Oevel, Gustaf met the love of his life, Josephine Daelemans.

Josephine was a bright and attractive woman of 19 years. Her father manufactured truck trailers and also ran a tavern in the larger town of Herentals. Like Gustaf, she came from a large family. In fact, with eleven brothers and sisters, Josephine's parents could not care adequately for all of the children. As was often the custom in those days, some children were sent to live temporarily with relatives. Josephine went to live with her grandmother in the town of Mol. Grandma owned a hardware store, and was financially able to send Josephine to a private school, where she learned to speak French almost as well as Flemish. Given her aforementioned attributes, Josephine was, naturally, popular with the young men. It was said that she also had an eye for handsome men herself.

One day as Josephine sat with her sister in a café in Herentals, they saw a young man ride up on his shiny Indian motorcycle. "Who's that?" Josephine asked, with obvious interest.

"Oh, that's *Stuf* Laenen," replied her sister, "he just returned from America!"

Josephine had once told her sister, "Someday, I am going to meet somebody who will take me to America." Now, she had the opportunity to meet a handsome and worldly man who could make her dreams come true. They were introduced, and immediately fell in love. Although Josephine was eleven years younger than Gustaf, she was taken with the ambitious young man and reveled in his stories of America. Within a year, they were married.

Gustaf and Josephine were married in January of 1925, and planned an immediate return to America. Gustaf told his wife of the opportunities in the new country and they agreed that they would raise their family in the United States. Their plans, however, were delayed for a couple of years when Gustaf was seriously injured in a motorcycle accident. Gustaf was an avid motorcyclist and, one day, crashed his beloved Indian motorcycle into a truck. He recovered from his injuries except for the damage done to his leg. For the rest of his life, he would walk with a limp, due to having one leg shorter than the other.

In some ways, Gustaf Laenen seemed destined to become an American. The ambitious young Belgian possessed many of the characteristics commonly associated with the American character. A strong spirit of independence and determination could be seen in his motorcycle riding adventures as well as in his choice to leave the security of a large family and community for the excitement and opportunity of a new country. That pioneering spirit would add yet another healthy strand to the fabric of America.

The unforeseen delay in emigrating meant that Gustaf and Josephine's first son would be born in Belgium, not the United States. Remie Laenen was born on April 18, 1926, in Oevel. While Gustaf was still recovering from his accident, in little more than a year the Laenens would realize their dream of immigrating to the United States. One-and-a-half-year-old Remie would soon steam into the

New York harbor with his parents, to see the Statue of Liberty for the first time. It would not be the last time.

Like most European immigrants, the Laenens came through Ellis Island, but this time, Gustaf did not go to Oregon. Instead, he and his young family settled on the east side of Detroit, Michigan, in a neighborhood where a substantial Belgian community had already been established.

The Belgians first came to Detroit in 1833 with the arrival of the Palms family from Antwerp. The patriarch of the Palms family was Ange Palms, who fought in Napoleon's army and, once established in Detroit, became one of the country's largest real estate and industrial tycoons of the time. Other Flemish families soon followed, and by the early 1920s there were about 7,000 Belgians living in the city, most in the east side neighborhood that sits between downtown Detroit and the neighboring upscale community of Grosse Pointe.

In addition to the Palms family (for whom the Palms Theatre and other local landmarks were named), there were many other Belgian families who made their mark in the Motor City. Peter DeCoster, who started the St. Vincent DePaul charitable society, came from Sint-Lievens-Esse in East Flanders in 1809. Charles Rabaut came to Detroit in 1848, and his grandson Louis C. Rabaut became a United States Congressman. All Belgians in the Detroit Area knew of Charlie Verheyden, who, prior to his death in 1985, built up one of the largest and most prestigious funeral home businesses in the country. A common joke among Belgians attending a funeral at Verheyden's was to comment "Don't look now, but I saw Charlie Verheyden sizing you up."

While it is impossible to make mention of every native Belgian who contributed to the local community, there are a few more names worth mentioning: The Dammans, the VanLerberghes, Charles Van de Poele, and the Verdonckts.

Adolph Damman opened his first hardware store in Detroit in 1920. He built up his business to become one of the largest independent hardware chains in Michigan. Adolph's son James was Lieutenant Governor of Michigan under William Milliken from 1974 until 1979.

Arthur J. VanLerberghe, like Charlie Verheyden, ran a highly successful funeral home business in the Detroit Area. Perhaps the most famous of the VanLerberghe customers was that of the Venerable Father Solanus Casey. Father Solanus was a monk at the St. Bonaventure Capuchin Monastery in Detroit, and is believed to have been associated with many miracles of healing, both during and after his time on earth. It is expected that the Catholic Church will, at some point in the near future, complete the process of declaring him to be a saint. The VanLerberghe family handled Father Solanus's funeral in 1957, and later his exhumation and reburial during the process of initiating his canonization.

Charles Van de Poele came to Detroit from Lichtervelde in 1868. While he was initially known for crafting high-quality furniture, he later made his mark as the inventor of the electric trolley (streetcar). A contemporary of Thomas Edison, he also brought electric lighting to the city of Detroit.

The Verdonckt family ran one of the best known bakeries in Detroit. Long after the population of Detroit migrated outward, many suburbanites would make the trip back into the city just for a tasty box of Verdonckt's special apricot squares.

These families by no means make up a complete or even representative list of the Belgian community in Detroit. These examples do, however, provide a sense of the strength of the Belgian community in Detroit at the time that Gustaf and Josephine Laenen brought their young family to live in America.

As was often the case for persons entering Ellis Island, Remie's name received a slight, but instant change upon his arrival into America. The Belgian spelling had always been Remi, after St. Remigius, the fifth century Archbishop of Rheims, but an Ellis Island clerk added an extra letter "e" to the end of his name. Remie kept that spelling, and has maintained it to this day.

By the time the Laenens arrived in Detroit, Josephine was already pregnant with their second child. The young family rented a room on Gladwin Street between Charlevoix and Goethe, in a boarding house that they shared with other people. At that time, even in America, most young families could not afford to own their own home. Those who could, often rented out rooms to augment their incomes.

Gustaf and Ray in 1927 at Rondele's grocery store in Detroit. Rondele's also sold malts and hops for local Belgian beer makers.

9

The Laenen's second child, Joseph, was born in October 1927. For the next seven years, the family took root in Detroit, and with each new day, became more and more American. In 1934, after seven years in the new country, Gustaf and Josephine became American citizens, and so, by process of derivation, did their two children. Today, as America receives almost daily criticism from much of the world and, indeed from within its own borders, it is perhaps helpful to recall that most people who immigrated to The United States stayed here. Later, Remie Laenen would recall that, "Both of my parents were very, very proud to be Americans. We were all fortunate to be Americans. I thank God that my father had the courage to leave his family and come over to this country. Because he had that courage, I was able to live here all of my life, and enjoy all of the privileges that come from being American."

Joe and Ray in wagon on Gladwin Street

At first, Gustaf took whatever part-time or temporary jobs he could find, mostly in small factories, and once in an ice warehouse. His injured leg made it difficult for him to perform some tasks, but he eventually landed a steady job as a metal finisher at the old Briggs Manufacturing plant on Mack Avenue.

The Laenens had become an average American family. All was not happy, however. A third son, named Frankie, was born on October 17, 1930 – three years to the day after Joseph - but died nine months later of a bowel obstruction. Gustaf and Josephine, who had themselves come from families of seventeen and eleven children, would have no more children.

Joe and Ray on Gladwin Street

In April 1934, Gustaf decided that he would take his family back to Belgium for a short visit. The visit lasted four months. It was not uncommon during the 1930s, for automobile and auto-related factories in Detroit to close for significant periods of time, because of lack of demand, or for extended re-tooling in preparation for changeover to the new models. Gustaf took advantage of this lay-off to make the trip back to Belgium. He and Josephine re-acquainted themselves with old friends and relatives, while their sons saw the land where their young lives had begun. They only needed to pay for the ship fare, as they were naturally welcomed to stay with relatives for free during the visit.

Scott Memorial Fountain
on Belle Isle.
Detroit, Mich, 1933

Laenens at Scott Fountain on Belle Isle, Detroit

Young Remie celebrated his eighth birthday in Oevel, Belgium. At first, he was quite dependent upon his parents for communication with the relatives. Josephine had shown a genuine knack for English, and had instilled in her sons an appreciation for both languages. Although he had been taught both English and Flemish at home, Remie was much less fluent in Flemish – at least at first. By the time he had returned home four months later, he recalled, "I had gotten so good at Flemish, that I could hardly speak English anymore!" Luckily, his English language skills returned in spades, and would serve him well for the rest of his life in America.

Chapter Two

A Good Catholic Education

By education, then, I mean goodness in the form in which it is first acquired by a child...the rightly disciplined state of pleasures and pains whereby a man from his first beginnings on will abhor what he should abhor and relish what he should relish
- Plato

Ray Laenen began his elementary education at the Lillibridge School in the Detroit Public Schools system. By the time he completed second grade, his parents, both devout Catholics, had decided to send the boys to a Catholic school. It might not have been a mere coincidence that the switch from public to Catholic schools occurred upon the family's return from their vacation in Belgium. Roman Catholicism is one of the uniting factors in the curiously divided country of Belgium. Although the country is geographically divided roughly in half between the majority Flemish to the north, and the French speaking Walloons to the south, the primary religion of all Belgians is, by far, Catholic.

Our Lady of Sorrows Catholic Church was historically considered to be "the Belgian church" in Detroit. Started in 1884, it has gone through several relocations and was last rebuilt after being destroyed by fire in 1963. The new church, dedicated in 1967, has primarily African American parishioners today, but remains a focal point for Belgians who often return to the church for special occasions. In the early 1930s however, the Laenen family lived a bit farther east, and closer to parishes of St. Bernard and St. Rose Catholic Churches.

In the fall of 1934, Remie and Joe began attending the St. Bernard Catholic School. They traded an environment of large classes, lay teachers and relatively casual dress, for one with nuns in habits, school uniforms, and classes the population of which you could almost count on two hands.

"Traffic Boys of St. Rose"

How the Laenen boys got into this particular school is, to this day, somewhat of a mystery. At the time, the family lived on Hillger Street near Goethe, which was the dividing line for the parishes of St. Bernard and St. Rose. Technically, the Laenens lived on the St. Rose side of the line, but attended St. Bernard because it was closer to their home. Two years later, it was discovered that the boys were attending the wrong school, and they were told that they would have to transfer to St. Rose in the following fall. This move would prove to be serendipitous for Ray Laenen.

Gustaf, Josephine and a neighbor (in the middle) on Hillger Street

In the fall of 1936, Remie Laenen entered the fifth grade at St. Rose School, which was located at the corner of Beniteau and Kercheval. The nuns who taught at St. Rose were of the Sisters, Servants of the Immaculate Heart of Mary (IHM) order, where the St. Bernard nuns had been Sisters of St. Joseph (SSJ). Some of the sisters whom Ray remembers from that period include Sr. Jane

Edward, Sr. Mary Catherine, Sr. Victoria, Sr. Leona and of course Mother Superior: Sister Mary Raymond. Over the years, the IHM nuns at St. Rose turned out some of the most prominent Detroiters including *Detroit Free Press* Publisher (retired) Neal Shine and auto dealer Jim Causley. It was in this fifth grade class that Remie met Tom Tschirhart.

St. Rose School (Photo courtesy of The Sisters, Servants of the Immaculate Heart of Mary)

At first, Tom Tschirhart and Remie Laenen had little in common, but in a school so small, the boys quickly became the best of friends. The two pals sat next to each other (or one behind the other) for all of their school years.

While Remie had emigrated from Belgium, Tom was born in the USA from parents of German descent. Where Remie played sports and loved athletics of all kinds, Tom was not the athletic type. Where

Remie's religious faith was ingrained in his personality, Tom tried his best to maintain high moral standards without taking all that religion stuff too seriously. Still, the two boys became inseparable – a distinction that would later prove to be more important than either boy could possibly have known at the time.

St. Rose Church was closed in 1989 and subsequently torn down (Photo courtesy of The Sisters, Servants of the Immaculate Heart of Mary)

Tom had been born just three days before Remie. The two boys hung out together both in and out of school. Their houses were not all that close together, as the Tschirharts lived a few blocks away on Montclair, south of Jefferson Avenue. All through grade school, the boys would make the daily trek to each other's home, until in high school they were able to "borrow" their parents' cars. Ray sheepishly admits that he didn't always quite have his father's permission to use the family's 1940 Buick sedan. But then, he never claimed to be a saint.

From this friendship, the Laenen and Tschirhart families also became friends, a bond that would continue throughout their lives. At the time, however, Tom and Ray had no idea of the sacrifices they would share in the future – in defense of the country they loved.

Ray remembers his parents as "a loving and affectionate couple." His mother was the disciplinarian of the family, but always in a warm and caring manner. Gustaf, a gentle man, was an easier mark for the boys to get what they wanted. Where Josephine would always ensure that Ray and Joe handled all of their chores, Gustaf was more likely to let a few things slide without losing any sleep over it. Despite their differences, both parents were well liked by family and friends. Gustaf smoked cigars, but his wife did not smoke – that is until Gustaf convinced her that she would look more stylish if she started to smoke cigarettes. All movie stars at the time seemed to look more sophisticated with a cigarette dangling from their hands. Josephine agreed, and took up the habit for the rest of her life, except for one period that will be discussed later.

During his years at St. Rose, Ray's parents maintained close relationships with many families in the Belgian-American community in Detroit. One wintry Saturday when Remie was twelve, the Laenens went to visit some friends at Gilbert's Bar. While Gustaf and Josephine socialized inside, Remie and Joe instigated a snowball fight outside with two younger girls they didn't know. One was named Lee, the niece of the bar owners, Mr. and Mrs. Gilbert, and the other was her cute little cousin, Norma DeMeulemeester. Norma, at ten years of age, made little impact on the twelve-year old Remie that day. Being two years younger, she was well off of his radar screen. But then, female intuition has always been much more accurate than radar. That day, having met Ray Laenen for the first time, Norma said to herself, "Someday, I'm going to marry that boy.

They would soon see each other again.

About a year and a half after the great snowball fight, the Laenen family went to the DeMeulemeester's home in nearby Grosse Pointe for a home cooked dinner. Memories being what they are, Ray remembers it to be a Mother's Day while Norma is sure that it was Thanksgiving. Regardless, the two snowball combatants met again.

Remie did not recognize the name DeMeulemeester, but as soon as he arrived at their home, he recognized the pretty young girl with whom he and his brother had traded snowballs a couple of years earlier. The now nearly teenaged Norma made a much better impact on the fourteen-year old Remie this time around. Norma recalls that when her parents told her that they had invited the Laenens for dinner, "A little bell went off, and I thought, 'I bet its those two guys." It certainly was.

Eventually, Ray and Norma would date a few times during high school, but never seriously. Remie remembers that they "went to a couple of proms, and maybe with a group of friends went over to Canada." That casual friendship would change significantly in just a few short years.

When Remie Laenen was fifteen, something else happened that would have a profound effect on his life – but he did not know it yet. Listening to the radio at home one Sunday morning – December 7, 1941, to be exact - he heard reports that Japanese aircraft had attacked an American naval base at Pearl Harbor, Hawaii. At first, he didn't know what to make of it. Hawaii was, after all, a long way from Detroit. He knew nothing at first of the scope of the attack or the extent of damage.

Later, as he drove with his parents down Lake Shore Drive toward the adjoining suburb of St. Clair Shores, he heard more details on the car radio. There had been massive damage to ships and airplanes, with many American casualties. It seemed now that war was about to be declared by our own country. The significance of this event was slowly beginning to register. Remie recalled that the more he heard on the radio, the more he realized that "This was a big, big thing!" Still, at fifteen, the likelihood that he would ever have to serve in this war seemed, at best, remote. After all, it was 1941, and he would not even be old enough to join the military until 1944. Surely, he thought, the war would be over by then.

Ray, Gustaf and Joe, "The Belgian Mafia."

From fifth grade to tenth grade at St. Rose, Remie Laenen and best friend Tom Tschirhart remained as conjoined twins of different mothers. The regimentation of a Catholic education was both predictable, and in Tom's mind, somewhat limiting. Just as, years before, Gustaf Laenen had left his home in search of a new world, Tom decided that St. Rose might just be a bit too limiting for two teenagers on the verge of manhood. The public schools, he thought, offered opportunities which were unavailable in the world of nuns, daily mass and uniform clothing. Tom had been entertaining ideas of becoming a pilot in the Army Air Corps, and wanted to improve his chances of acceptance by taking advantage of the more advanced algebra and geometry classes offered at the much larger public high school. The public school system also seemed to offer a student more autonomy than was offered in the Catholic schools.

"You could pick and choose your classes easier at Southeastern," said Tom, "where at St. Rose, the curriculum was more determined for you."

In the summer after tenth grade, Tom decided that for the next semester he would leave the nuns behind and enroll in the Detroit Public Schools. Ray was not so sure that this was a good idea, but in the interest of a long-term friendship, he allowed himself to be convinced that this was the thing to do. He broke the news to his parents and they essentially told him that he was old enough to make his own decisions.

With the implicit permission of his parents, and the headstrong resolve of a teenager, Ray left the IHM sisters behind and enrolled in Detroit Southeastern High School for his junior year. It didn't take much time for Tom and he to realize that they had made a big mistake. From a school where all of the teachers and other students knew their names, they had now entered the gigantic and (in comparison) anonymous vortex of the Detroit Public Schools. To Remie, it felt as if he had gone from an elementary school to a university.

This was not the worst of it. While Tom had engaged in few extracurricular activities at St. Rose, Ray played sports year round. He had excelled at football, baseball, and basketball. After he had transferred to Southeastern, he discovered that eligibility rules would prohibit him from playing any sports until he had completed one year at the new school. He was crestfallen, but it was too late to go back.

Realizing their mistake, both boys completed the semester at Southeastern, and then returned to St. Rose for their senior year with a lesson learned. Even back at the Catholic school, however, Remie discovered that he would have to wait out one more semester to become eligible to play sports again. He completely missed football, but was able to play half the basketball season, and all of the next baseball season.

As World War II raged on, the Laenen family worried about their relatives who were still living in Belgium. The Nazis had marched through Oevel on their way to Holland, and once again, Belgium was forced to acquiesce to hostile neighbors. In addition to the ever-present fear for life, limb and safety, it was known that the Nazis had forced some Belgians to work in locally constructed concentration camps and in German factories. Even Belgium's King Leopold III had been temporarily sent into exile in Switzerland.

Like a self-fulfilling prophecy, Gustaf once again felt the old conflict about being away from his family during a time of need. Ray remembers that "It tugged at my father's heart to know that *they* were there, and there was nothing he could do." Strangely, Ray does not remember the nuns of St. Rose talking much about the war. He recalls that they just continued doing what they did, teaching the children about arithmetic, history and religion.

The Belgian community in Detroit, like everyone else, made sacrifices for the war. The Laenens had a very nice victory garden in the back yard. Ray remembers that his father "always had good gardens" attributable in large part to his farming background.

"Gas and rubber rationing curtailed the driving," remembered Ray, "although not necessarily in equal proportion for every family." The DeMeulemeester's family-owned saloon, it seems, was located directly across from a gas station at Warren Avenue and St. Jean Street. Apparently, Mr. DeMeulemeester had worked out some sort of quid pro quo arrangement with the gas station owner. Mr. D was able to get gas or tires as he needed, and conversely, the gas station owner could get himself filled up at the bar - also as needed. Despite such exceptions, Ray looks at the obvious difference in sacrifices between that war and the current war in Iraq. In today's war, unless you have a friend or family member who is serving in the Middle East, the difference in our lives is barely noticeable. "People today," says Ray, "don't know what sacrifice is when it comes to war."

The big war had far reaching effects on the psyche of all Americans. When Gustaf's father died in Belgium of natural causes in 1944, Ray felt certain that his grandfather's death had to be somehow connected to the war. He felt angry towards the "Germans and Italians, who had caused so much trouble in Europe," and thought that maybe his grandfather had caught pneumonia or some other illness because they didn't have enough heat or medicine due to the war. Soon, Remie would get his chance to do what his father could not do, help out both of his countries – Belgium and the United States of America.

At the time, Ray could not have known or appreciated the value of that St. Rose education. Like the others in his class, he learned how to read, write and spell. His handwriting – forged at the careful hands of the Sisters of the Immaculate Heart of Mary - is, to this day, exemplary. He acquired knowledge of mathematics, history and geography that would form a solid cornerstone for a lifetime of learning.

Ray and Friends on graduation day 1944

Ray on graduation day 1944

He also learned about faith. For some, a Catholic education is like a shackle to be cut off and discarded once one has tasted the freedom of the outside world. For Ray Laenen, it was more like a preparatory academy that girded him in the armor of faith. It was well fitting armor that would serve him gloriously for a lifetime. At one point after Ray had returned from military service, Father Emmett Hannick, Ph.D., who was pastor of St. Rose, sent Ray a letter in which he urged him to consider joining the priesthood. The priest recognized in Ray, a larger well of faith than that of the average man. Also, he felt that God must have spared Ray's life that night of February 6, 1945 for a good reason. Perhaps, thought Father Hannick, Ray was destined to be a priest. Ray seriously considered the vocation, but ultimately decided to remain a man of faith, but not of the cloth. Still, his faith remained strong throughout his life. In good times and in bad, Ray's faith in God was unshakeable.

Father Hannick (Photo courtesy of the Archdiocese of Detroit)

Chapter Three

A Time to Serve

Boot, saddle, to horse, and away!
– Robert Browning

T hree weeks after he graduated from St. Rose High School, Ray Laenen entered the United States Army. The route to his induction was somewhat circuitous. Ray knew that as soon as he graduated from high school, he would receive a draft notice, and he did. His first thought was to become a pilot.

He first tried to join the Naval Air Force and then the Army Air Corps, but was rejected by both because he was color blind. Even in wartime, when the need for combat personnel was strongest, our military wisely understood that a colorblind flier would be at best, at a distinct disadvantage, and at worst, a possible hindrance to the cause. No matter, Ray would still do his part. He was drafted into the army and was inducted on July 13, 1944. Ray's parents expected this day to come, and bravely gave him their support – and prayers.

Mike Keegan, a friend who would later become Ray's brother-in-law, gave him a small silver religious medal to take with him wherever he would go. He immediately placed the medal on the chain next to his dogtag. It had several iconic images on the front, and the back was inscribed with the words: *I am a catholic...please call a priest.* Throughout the tribulations that would follow, the medal never left that strong chain around Ray's neck. It remains in his possession today, a reminder of both his faith in God, and his service to America.

The medal that Ray wore around his neck – front view

Medal – back view

The new recruits pose for a group portrait at Fort Sheridan.

From the day he was inducted, until the day of his discharge two years later, Ray's mother wrote to him every day. *Every day*! Some of the letters reached Ray many weeks after they were written, but he eventually got them all. Ray, being the temporary property of the United States Army, was not able to respond to each letter. He did, however, write back as often as he could, and for all the time he was in the service, sent telegrams to his parents on Mother's Day and Father's Day.

Not surprisingly, friend Tom Tschirhart was inducted on the same day, and the two teenagers reported together to Fort Sheridan, Illinois for processing. They hoped that the army would keep them together at least through basic training, but each knew that, as Ray stated, "The Army tells you where to go, you don't tell them!"

Ray and Tom did, however, remain together. After induction, they were transferred to Fort Riley, Kansas, for basic training, where they were offered a choice – they could either sign up for the mechanized infantry or for the cavalry. Their options would be tanks or horses. Recalling their previous ill-fated decision to transfer to Southeastern High School, the two young men did not want to make the wrong choice this time. It seemed to them that tanks or any other armed vehicles would surely put them directly in harms way much more than would horses. They were surprised that the U.S. Army still had a cavalry division, more of a throwback to the days of General Custer, than to General Patton. Neither Ray nor Tom had had much experience riding horses, but discretion being the better part of valor, they decided to join the cavalry – Troop X, 1st Regiment. The drill sergeant told them not to worry, "In seventeen weeks, you'll know how to ride a horse."

Private Laenen at parade rest, Fort Riley

Fort Riley was a perfect place for the Cavalry Replacement Training Center (CRTC). Given its location in the flatlands of Kansas, it was surprisingly hilly with woods, water and rocky slopes. The CRTC offered cavalry trainees a wide variety of terrain on which to hone their equestrian skills. Fort Riley has, in fact, been around since 1853, and has an illustrious history. It has, at different times, been home to several noted cavalry regiments including General George Custer's 7th Cavalry Regiment, and the various African American regiments known collectively as the Buffalo Soldiers.

It was during his stay at Ft. Riley that Private Remie Laenen had his name fined-tuned once more to meet American tastes. Having been tweaked first at Ellis Island (from Remi to Remie) his colleagues and superiors at Ft. Riley now decided that he would simply be called *Ray*. Apparently the two-syllable *Remie* did not fit with the casual American camaraderie of the 1st Regiment, and so the second syllable was unceremoniously lopped off. As before, Ray adapted to the change without missing a beat, and kept the nickname for the rest of his life. Today, in an age where multiculturalism and diversity are the zeitgeist, it is perhaps helpful to remember that assimilation is actually the backbone of a tolerant society. Without assimilation, we run the risk of degenerating into the tribal and Balkanized societies in which most of the world's conflicts are spawned today. It was a simple thing, but another indication of Ray's powerful desire to fit into American culture.

The official motto of the U.S. Cavalry is *"Hit the leather and ride."* And ride they did, day in and day out. Ray was assigned a horse named Blitz. Blitz was a regal looking mare with an excellent disposition. She would be Ray's perfect partner in training for the next seventeen weeks.

Ray Laenen atop his horse Blitz

All soldiers have a colorful drill sergeant whom they will remember for the rest of their days. For the men of the CRTC, it was Sergeant Zaleski. Sergeant Zaleski ensured that the men stayed on task. One day, Ray recalls, the men were out on a long ride. Sergeant Zaleski noticed that some of the soldiers did not appear to be taking his riding lessons quite as seriously as he had intended. He stopped the offending riders (which included Privates Tschirhart and Laenen) and addressed the group.

"Alright you guys, so you think this is a big joke?"

Their denials did nothing to dissuade the sergeant from the retribution that was to come.

"OK," he said, "I want each of you to take your stirrups and cross them over the top of the animal to the other side."

This, of course would prevent the men from using the stirrups to brace their tender bottoms against the jostling of their horses over the rough terrain. He made them ride that way for what seemed like a half-hour, until the men learned their lesson – by the seats of their pants.

The cavalry soldiers also learned the proper way to pack a horse. There were several different ways to do it, depending on the type of supplies to be carried. They learned to load a horse with a machine gun, bazooka, food, ammunition and other war materiel. They were never trained to ride or load mules, but the army figured that if you know how to ride and pack a horse, you will be able to do the same with a mule.

The men also learned how to ride properly and to take care of their assigned horses. They were responsible for all of the horses' care except for shoeing. That task was left to the professionals. They learned to clean the horses' hooves, and made sure that the animals were properly fed and groomed. They learned to ride with their heels down, knees locked into the horse's body, and with the balls of their feet in the stirrups (except when ordered by Sgt. Zaleski to do otherwise).

Ray and Tom made many new friends among the recruits. Many of these men came from Detroit, or surrounding areas of Michigan. When you are away from home for the first time, anyone with even a slight connection to your hometown or state becomes a friend. They met one soldier who had gone to Southeastern High School – where Ray and Tom had spent that one ill-fated semester. His name was Chuck Briley, and he would later join them on their first mission aboard the *SS Peter Silvester.*

Ray remembers Chuck as "…a good guy, tall, blond and friendly." But Ray and Tom would sometimes become a little irritated at him, because he would never stop talking about his girlfriend back home. "It was always 'Marie this' and 'Marie that' and 'when I get back to Marie'" said Ray, "and we kind of got tired of hearing him talk about her all the time." Both Chuck Briley and his girl Marie would later provide some unexpected and memorable moments in Ray Laenen's life.

From left: Tom Morawski, "Mac" McLean, Ray, and Tom Tschirhart. Bill Furlage kneeling in front

There was another local man in the 1st Regiment from Kalamazoo, Michigan named Tom Spicketts. Like Remie Laenen, Spicketts had his original surname Americanized upon his family's entry into this country. The very Italian Spicuzza name had instantly been transformed into the more easily pronounced Spicketts. And there was yet another Tom, Tom Morawski from St.Philip School on the east side of Detroit. These five men from Michigan – Ray Laenen, Chuck Briley, and *The Three Toms* – took to calling each other *Amigo*. The five Amigos would form a bond of friendship that would continue beyond the CRTC, leaving indelible marks on the souls of each man.

Ray and Tom Morawski in back, unidentified soldiers in front

Tom Tschirhart recalls one incident at Fort Riley that will remain in his memory forever. One day, Ray's brother Joe, and another friend from St. Rose came to visit Tom and Ray in boot camp. Naturally, being away from their parents for the first time in their lives, the young men decided to go out and cut loose a little bit. The newly emancipated young Turks drank beer and smoked cigarettes all night long. This would not be unusual except for the fact that Ray was neither a drinker nor a smoker. As Tom now describes the night,

"Now you know that Ray doesn't drink and doesn't smoke. But I've seen him drunk and smoking at the same time!" Tom takes a certain amount of glee in relating that story as he knows that he witnessed a rare moment of abandon in the life of an otherwise unwaveringly moderate man.

Tom Tschirhart, Fuller Brush Man

In November 1944, Tom Tschirhart and Ray Laenen completed their basic training and were given a ten-day furlough to go back home to Detroit. They enjoyed seeing their families again, and proudly strutted around in their new army uniforms. Their enjoyment and bravado helped to mask their fears about where they would go from here. They knew that when they returned from furlough, they would each be given their first combat orders. A soldier never knows ahead of time where he will be going, but Ray thought that there was a very good chance that they would be sent to Europe, and quite possibly to the very place where he was born, Belgium. As Ray would later reminisce, "Here I was, born in Belgium, grew up in the United States, went into the Army, and could have been shipped back to Belgium where I might have lost my life in the land of my birth."

On furlough visiting his parents

Big brother Ray home on furlough

At that time, in November 1944, the war in Belgium and France was all but over – or so everyone thought. Beginning with the D-Day invasion of Normandy, France on June 6, 1944, the Allied forces had systematically beaten the German Army back from front after front, leading to the German forces' retreat from France and Belgium. The Germans were essentially holed up in their homeland as Allied forces planned the eventual assault into Germany itself. Clearly the tide was turning in favor of the Allies, but Hitler had one last surprise up his sleeve.

On December 16, 1944, the Germans launched one last massive assault on the Allied forces who were scattered within the Ardennes Forest of Belgium near the town of Bastogne. This would become known as the Battle of the Bulge, as it was Hitler's intent to breach the line held by Allied defenses. Although it came late in the war, it would turn out to be the largest battle of WWII on European soil. Over a million soldiers took part in the Battle of the Bulge, with each side suffering thousands of casualties. When it was over, the Germans held no more territory than they had held before the battle, but their strength was severely weakened for the remainder of the war. But in November 1944, the outcome in Europe was still uncertain. Ray and Tom were convinced that, upon their return from furlough, they would be sent to the European front.

As it turned out, Ray and Tom were not sent to Belgium, or for that matter even to Europe. When they returned from furlough, they were sent to Fort Ord, California. They knew that they were about to be put into service somewhere, but still had no idea where they were going.

At Fort Ord, Ray met a couple more Michigan men. Don Tuthill and Chuck Kemmer had also trained at Fort Riley, but were in a different troop than Ray and the Three Toms. Although they didn't know each other much at the time, these two men would later share some experiences with Ray that would bind their friendships for life. Apparently, Ray made quite an impression on all of his buddies. Kemmer recalls that Ray was well liked by everyone: "He was ...and still is... such a nice guy to talk to, and he was very entertaining." This sentiment was echoed by virtually all of the men that Ray served with. Tom Spicketts remembers that "Ray had a lot of friends. He was a squad leader and everybody respected him. Of course, he respected everyone else too, and made each person feel that they were special."

One evening, a sergeant at Ft. Ord whom Ray did not know, mentioned that he had access to everyone's orders and "for a couple of bucks each" would tell each of them where they would be going. Anxious to sate their curiosity, Ray and Tom Tschirhart paid the money to the sergeant. He said that he would check the records that night and let them know in the morning where they would be going. Of course, that was the last they ever saw of the sergeant - or their money. Another lesson learned.

After only one week at Ft. Ord, they were again transferred, this time to Santa Ana, California, where they finally learned their true mission. They would sail on a Liberty Ship from Santa Ana, California, to Melbourne, Australia, and then on to Colombo, Ceylon (now Sri Lanka) with a cargo of 317 mules. From there, they would take the mules to Calcutta, India and on into the torrid jungles of Burma where they would join their Allied brothers' struggle against the Japanese.

Strangely, after all of that training, they would not take their horses with them. After spending seventeen weeks with their horses, all of the men had to bid goodbye to their equine companions, never to see them again. Ray recalled "Blitz was my partner for seventeen weeks. It hurt to leave that horse." It seemed wasteful, but apparently the men were needed for something else. On New Year's Eve, 1944, Ray Laenen and Tom Tschirhart boarded the *SS Peter Silvester* for a journey that they never could have imagined back at old St. Rose.

Chapter Four

Why They Needed Mules in Burma

The mules greatly objected to being jabbed or prodded in the process of loading a piece of the gun on their backs. Even being the proper height, this sometimes did occur and the consequences could be severe.
– Kenneth E. Laabs (a soldier in the 612th Field Artillery Battalion)

While many Americans tend to think of December 7, 1941, the day the Japanese attacked Pearl Harbor, as the beginning of World War II for the United States, Japan had actually sown the seeds of war much earlier. In 1931, Japan had taken over the Chinese region of Manchuria in an effort to expand its overpopulated land base, steal China's natural resources, and eventually become the dominant power of the massive Asian continent. Emboldened by its success in Manchuria, Japan continued to expand its military conquest of China. By 1937 (while Ray Laenen and Tom Tschirhart were still students at St. Rose) Japan had occupied enough Chinese cities to have essentially formed a protective barrier between the Chinese mainland and the rest of the world.

The year 1937 marked the beginning of a war between China and Japan that would eventually lead to China's alliance with the United States, Great Britain and the other Allied powers in World War II. But Japan was not content to simply grab parts of China. It had also planned to conquer all of the neighboring countries of Southeast Asia, and had almost succeeded. By 1942, in addition to Manchuria and parts of China, the Japanese had already captured Thailand, French Indochina (now primarily Cambodia, Laos and Viet Nam), Malaya, Korea, Sumatra, the Philippines, Burma and virtually every island between Australia and Asia.

As Japan consumed country after country in that area, Germany was doing the same to its neighboring countries in Europe. This unholy alliance of two powers bent on world domination produced the Axis, which would draw the major world powers into the greatest war of all time.

Of particular interest to Ray Laenen's future, was the area of conflict known to the Allies as the China-Burma-India (CBI) Theater of Operations. With limited resources spread thin all over the world, the CBI Theater was determined by the Allies to be of lesser importance than the battles being fought in Europe and the Pacific. For that reason, both troops and supplies were in very short supply, while the Japanese pressed on relentlessly in their quest to conquer Southeast Asia. Despite its "low-priority" status, the CBI Theater produced some of the most colorful and memorable military figures and units of the war, including General "Vinegar Joe" Stilwell, The

Flying Tigers, Merrill's Marauders, the Mars Task Force, and British General Orde Wingate's *Chindits*.

Geographically, the (then) British colony of Burma fit like a jigsaw puzzle piece between the southwestern edge of China and the southeastern border of India. This made Burma essential to the Japanese plans to take over China. By May 1942, the Japanese had already taken Burma and driven the Allies out of the country in one of the most humiliating defeats we would experience during the war. General "Vinegar Joe" Stilwell, led as many Allied troops as possible to safety in India, but vowed to come back and avenge this horrific loss.

General Stilwell retreats from Burma in 1942
(Photo courtesy of the National Archives)

Even before the United States had entered the war, it had "lent" a group of rough and tumble volunteer fighter pilots to China under the supervision of American General Claire Chennault. This squadron, known as "The Flying Tigers" painted the noses of their near obsolete

Curtiss P-40 Tomahawk fighter planes with menacing shark teeth, and went on to score many victories against the far superior Japanese Zero aircraft. They kept the Japanese from further incursions into China, and after the United States entered the war, were legitimized as the Army's 14th Air Force.

From 1942 until the end of the war in 1945, Burma remained a key territory for both the Allies and the Axis forces. Japan needed to retain as much of the land it had appropriated as possible, and Burma, given its location between China and India, was central to this defense.

The Allies needed to regain control of Burma as a means to ensure that a sufficient amount of military supplies could get through to China. With the Japanese in control of Burma, the Allies had no reliable means of transporting supplies over ground routes. All transport of supplies at that time relied on air shipments over a dangerous section of the Himalayas known as "The Hump" which was marked by violently high winds and, at times, monsoon rains. This air route which went from the province of Assam, India to Kunming, China, was so dangerous that over the course of the war, over 850 airmen lost their lives flying supplies over The Hump. In addition to the danger of flying huge C-46 and C-47 cargo planes, air transport was limited to the small size cargo loads that could be carried under such conditions. Where a converted C-46 (they were previously used as commercial luxury airliners) could carry only about four tons of cargo per trip, a fully laden sea vessel could deliver 10,000 tons of cargo per trip, for eventual ground transport. Clearly, a ground route from India to China was needed.

The Burma Road was an ancient passage, which traversed the area between Kunming, China into what was now Japanese occupied Burma. Parts of the road were nearly two thousand years old but had been improved and expanded as the dark clouds of war moved across Southeast Asia in 1938/1939. Still, in order to secure a supply route, the Allies would need to build a whole new road through the mountainous jungles of Burma, from Ledo, India to the existing Burma Road at Bhamo, India, thus providing a direct ground link between India and China. General "Vinegar Joe" Stilwell was put in charge of the project.

The Burma Road winds through the mountainside
(Photo courtesy of the National Archives)

The construction of the Ledo road was controversial from the beginning, with many British and American leaders seriously doubting that the project could be completed in time to be of any benefit to the war effort. Adding to the controversy, was the fact that the cantankerous Stilwell, a notoriously tactless straight shooter who once publicly called Chaing Kai Shek "stupid and gutless," was repeatedly garnering the contempt of China's leader. Despite his stellar reputation as a soldier and military strategist, Stilwell's personality got in the way so often that he was eventually re-assigned from the project that bore his name. Despite the lack of full support from the Allied command, construction of the road was started in 1942. Known variously as the Ledo Road, the Ledo-Burma road or Stilwell Road, it served as an important means of incursion into Japanese-occupied Burma.

As roads go, the Ledo and Burma roads were not exactly superhighways. The gravel and compacted sand surface of the roads were certainly an improvement over the rocky cliffs and thick sodden jungle over which they were built. Monsoon rains and other impediments, however, would make the roads treacherous and, at times, impassable. For this reason, mules became an indispensable element for the soldiers along the Burma and Ledo Roads.

Mules were essential to both the road-building crews and the combat soldiers fighting within the units known as Merrill's Marauders, Wingate's Chindits and the Mars Task Force. The mules could go where military trucks, half-tracks and even jeeps could not. Mules were used to transport supplies for the Allied and Chinese soldiers leaving Burma after the 1942 defeat, and then for their return to the subsequent road-building and later combat activities. All ground troops who served in CBI could, to a certain extent, thank the mules for playing a major part in their survival and eventual success in this region. Clearly, they also owed a debt of gratitude to the men who transported the mules across enemy infested oceans aboard various Liberty Ships.

Merrill's Marauders guide horses and mules over the Ledo Road
(Photo courtesy of the National Archives)

General Orde Wingate was a walking archetype of the eccentric British officer. Favoring a WWI pith helmet and a disheveled hodgepodge of clothing over the more modern uniform of the WWII fighting soldier, he was known far and wide as being, well, *a bit daft* as the Brits might say. Like the American General George Patton, he was known to occasionally strike one of his own men, but unlike Patton, he had a few slightly more *unusual* habits. Wingate was a bright and well-read man (he was known to quote both Plato and the Bible in the same breath) who strained his tea through his socks – and then served that tea to his guests. The tea, however, was probably the least of his guests concerns, as he often liked to entertain his friends while stark naked.

General Orde Wingate, fully clothed
(Photo courtesy of the United States Air Force)

Despite his peculiarities, Wingate assembled a fearsome band of guerilla jungle fighters who became known as "The Chindits", a mispronunciation of the *chinthe* or sculpted lions which guarded the Burmese temples. Wingate's Chindits not only proved their mettle in battling the Japanese, but they also trained their American counterparts who fought as the 5307th Composite Unit (Provisional). These men would become known as The Galahad Force, or more commonly, *Merrill's Marauders*, for the man under whom they served: Brigadier General Frank D. Merrill. One measure of their extraordinary success was the outcome of one battle in which the Marauders reportedly killed over 800 Japanese soldiers, but lost only eight men of their own.

The soldiers of the Mars Task Force finally routed the Japanese from the Burma Road for good in October 1944. This group of men were the successors to Merrill's Marauders, and, like the others, owed a good part of their success to the mules which were shipped to their units by men like Ray Laenen.

Ken Laabs, of Kalama, Washington, was a member of the 612th Field Artillery Battalion, which was part of the Mars Task Force. His experiences provide a rare first hand glimpse of what it was like to fight the Japanese in the jungles of Burma, and on into China. Laabs' unit traversed over 800 miles of mountainous jungle, with 75mm Howitzers strapped to the backs of their mules. This means of transportation allowed them to travel off roads, where the Japanese could not, thereby giving the Americans a distinct "high ground" advantage.

In one of those logistical curiosities that most of us would never think to consider, the men who were assigned to the 612th were required to be of a certain height – so that they could easily load the seven heavy pieces of the Howitzer on to a mule's back. Ken Laabs recalls, "Before leaving our basic training camps, we were checked for height. If you did not exceed five-foot ten, or five-foot eleven inches, you were not one of the "lucky ones" who went to Camp Gruber."

Men of the Mars Task Force
(Photo courtesy of the National Archives)

Mules that did not carry guns, carried food, grain or ammunition. Unfortunately, like many other war resources, the supply of mules would often be reduced by attrition from several sources. "...Many mules fell with their loads into the deep ravines (Laabs, pg. 22)." Others sunk in mud, and could not be pulled out. Another unit had to destroy all of its mules because the animals contracted a contagious blood disease. Even Merrill's Marauders were not immune from the problem of mule attrition: "In a single exasperating day, the 3rd Battalion lost 20 mules, and was forced to leave behind some 4000 pounds of sorely needed equipment. Only half the pack animals survived the trek to Myitkyina (Moser, pg128)." The importance of the mules to the CBI theater of operations was summed up in a sardonic joke made by some of the British soldiers, who said that the Distinguished Combat Medal, or DCM, actually stood for: *Died Chasing Mules* (Moser).

One final note on the importance of the mules. It has been reported that the food supplies were in such grave shortage at times, that some Allied soldiers were forced to eat their own mules to survive (Moser). Clearly, the mules were as essential to the CBI Theater as were the tanks and Jeeps in Europe.

While the Mars Task Force had taken back the Burma Road by October 1944, the war was not over for either Ken Laabs or for Ray Laenen. The Mars force would continue to press on into China pushing the Japanese back out of the remaining areas they continued to occupy. Meanwhile, the Allied forces were planning a major offensive into Japanese held Eastern China in the spring of 1945. For this, they would need more mules.

Chapter Five

The Liberty Ships

Here is the answer which I will give to President Roosevelt...Give us the tools, and we will finish the job.
– Winston Churchill

D uring World War II, the Axis and Allied forces each depended on strong supply lines to provide the resources necessary to accomplish their military objectives. Without an adequate means of supplying the food, weapons, ammunition and medical supplies necessary for war, even the most carefully planned strategic operations would be doomed to failure. There was a major difference, however, between the supply needs of the Axis forces, and those of the Allied forces. Japan, Germany, and to a lesser extent Italy, were for the most part, fighting outward from central, home-based locations. This meant that the vast majority of their war supplies could be transported without interruption over land routes, or if by sea, at least through non-hostile waters. For the Allies, transportation of war materials presented a different and much more formidable task.

The Allied nations were spread out over five continents: Asia, Europe, North America Australia, and parts of Africa. Although the primary battlefronts were on the continents of Europe and Asia, the countries located on those shores did not have the resources necessary to defend themselves alone. This meant that natural and manufactured goods (not to mention personnel) had to be shipped from North America, South America, and Australia to the fighting fronts in Europe and Asia. Old maritime shipping routes now became military lifelines.

Prior to the attack on Pearl Harbor, many in the United States had been reluctant to enter the war. Just as now, where there are those who feel that the United States has no need for direct involvement in Middle Eastern conflicts, many at that time adhered to a similar isolationist position - believing that this was not *our* war. Nonetheless, through the initial "cash-and-carry" program and later, the more official Lend-Lease program, the United States sent war materials to the British who had already depleted much of their military and cash reserves in the fight against Nazi Germany. Even prior to our declaration of war in December 1941, American warships were put into action to protect the convoys of supply ships steaming across the Atlantic Ocean - enroute to our good friend and ally Great Britain.

A convoy of supply ships including several Liberty Ships, 1944
(Photo courtesy of Library of Congress)

Unfortunately, Hitler understood all too well the importance of these supply routes between allies. German U-boats were dispatched to the Atlantic to sink as many Allied supply ships as possible, thereby crippling the lifeblood of the Allied defense. Initially, they were quite successful. The early losses in British and American merchant shipping vessels were staggering: "During those first twelve months of the war, a total of 385 British ships amounting to 1.7 million gross tons, 10 per cent of the September 1939 total, had been lost, primarily as the result of the German U-boat campaign (Elphick, pg. 12)."

The German U-boats were, in fact, sinking British merchant ships three times faster than the British could replace them. Churchill begged the United States to help out, knowing that if Britain fell, only the Atlantic Ocean would separate America from a German war machine bent on world domination. A plan was soon developed that would merge a British design for a useful merchant ship with the American resources and manufacturing muscle necessary to get the job done on a large scale.

In order to understand the nature of the Liberty Ship, one must first understand its purpose. Louis Henri Sullivan's dictum that *form ever follows function*, was never so true as in the development of the Liberty Ships. Put bluntly, the Liberty Ship project was initiated as a means to build merchant shipping vessels faster than Hitler's U-boats could sink them. This meant that the speed and quantity of production were more important than the quality of the ships themselves. The Allies needed a lot of ships fast, and not necessarily of the latest or best design. This didn't mean that quality would be purposely sacrificed at the expense of the safety of crew and cargo, but if the needed quantity of supplies did not get through to the Allied war effort, no amount of quality in shipbuilding would be of any consequence. For that reason, the ships were considered to be "emergency vessels" with all necessary efficiencies of design and construction to meet the immediate goal or function: that of producing as many ships as possible in as short a time as possible. A congressional committee on the emergency shipbuilding program concluded, "The design is the best that can be devised for an emergency product to be quickly, cheaply and simply built (Elphick, pg. 65)."

*Laying the keel of a Liberty Ship at Bethlehem Fairfield Shipyard, 1943
(Photo courtesy of Library of Congress)*

The first efficiency was to borrow an existing design rather than develop a new one. An old design (with some elements dating back to the Nineteenth Century) from the Joseph L. Thompson & Sons Shipbuilding Company in England was given expeditious modifications and pressed into service. The actual construction of the ships would be done in the United States by any of about eighteen different shipyards – some of which had already existed, and others, which had to be built strictly for this purpose.

On the twenty-fourth day, the ship is ready for launching
(Photo courtesy of Library of Congress)

The first and most prominent name associated with the building of Liberty Ships is that of Henry J. Kaiser. Kaiser was an industrialist who had already overseen the completion of several large construction and engineering projects, including the Boulder Dam. He would later build his short-lived *Henry J* automobile at the same Willow Run, Michigan, factory where the Ford Motor Company had built World War II bombers. Kaiser's proven track record instilled in congress the confidence that he would be able to get the project launched quickly.

The second efficiency was the application of modern manufacturing techniques to the previous and somewhat anachronistic unit-by-unit shipbuilding methods. Sections of the Liberty Ship were built separately (sometimes offsite), and then assembled to the keel structure like a gargantuan automobile on the assembly line. This method greatly expedited the construction process, and allowed many parts to be manufactured simultaneously in different locations.

The third efficiency was in the copious use of welding in place of the more common riveting process used in most other ship construction. This use of welding was to come under criticism later for its perceived role in the structural failures of an inordinate number of Liberty Ships. It was thought (erroneously) that the welded ships may have had weaker seams than the riveted ships of similar design, and would break apart in rough seas or upon a torpedo attack that – some assumed – would have done less damage to a riveted ship. Peter Elphick, in his exhaustive review, has concluded that although the exact cause of all Liberty Ship failures can not be entirely determined, it would appear that causes other than welding were more often to blame. While the welded ships may have broken up slightly more frequently in cold weather than the riveted ships, the problem seems to have been more with the type of steel used in these vessels than with the method of assembly: "The problem was not riveting vs welding, but ductile steel vs notch sensitive steel (Elphick, pg. 171)."

Welding a Liberty Ship (Photo courtesy of Library of Congress)

It is often repeated these days, that the efficiency of the American Liberty Ship building program was such that by the end of the war, a new Liberty Ship could be built in only four days. This is, for the most part, a myth. In truth, at the beginning of the project, the *SS Patrick Henry*, the first Liberty Ship built, took about five months to complete. By the end of the war, that build time had been reduced to an average of less than forty days per ship. While still an impressive feat, it does not compare to the one event that gave rise to the legend of the four-day Liberty Ship.

Workers built the *SS Robert E. Peary* at one of Kaiser's shipyards in the astounding time of exactly four days, fifteen hours, and twenty-nine seconds (Elphick)! This was not, however, the norm. The *Peary* was built as an exercise to build morale among the shipyard workers, and to send a message to the Germans and Japanese about the Allied Forces' manufacturing prowess. In order to accomplish this Herculean task, crews and equipment were taken off of virtually every other ship in the yard so that all of the resources of that shipyard could be applied to the rapid completion of this one ship. Regardless of the motivation, it was an incredible accomplishment, not likely to be bested anytime soon, if ever.

Virtually all of the Liberty Ships were built to the same design. Each hull was approximately 441 feet long and 56 feet wide. Power was provided by a couple of 2,500-horsepower steam engines, which burned fuel oil to create the steam. They could carry about 9,000 tons of cargo in the five holds, but could also carry a great deal more on deck, depending on how the ship was trimmed out. This translated into a huge amount of cargo carrying capacity – especially in comparison the amount that could be flown over the hump in any single trip. All told, "A Liberty could carry 2,840 jeeps, 440 tanks, or 230 million rounds of rifle ammunition (www.USMM.org)."

The Liberty Ships were by no means battle ships, but given that they were to transport troops and supplies through hostile waters, they came equipped with several guns. Most ships carried eight 20mm anti-aircraft guns and one or two three-inch guns fore and aft. This armament differed only slightly from ship to ship. Because most of the Liberty Ship crews were made up of some combination of merchant seaman and army soldiers, the task of manning the guns fell to the Naval Armed Guard. Each Liberty Ship had about twenty-five Armed Guard personnel assigned to defend the ship from enemy attack. Sadly, however, the ships did not carry depth charges, and so were quite vulnerable to attacks from German U-boats.

Exactly 2,710 Liberty Ships were built by eighteen American shipyards during the war. At first, most of the ships were named after prominent figures in American history such as the appropriately named *SS Patrick Henry* ("Give me liberty or give me death!").

Eventually, given the sheer volume of ships and the need for money to build them, the government began to name ships in honor of any deceased American for whom a substantial amount of money could be raised in his or her name. This led to a rich assortment of ship names, the likes of which this country has never seen. There were ships named after frontiersmen Davey Crockett, Daniel Boone, Jim Bowie and Kit Carson. Some of the great American artists who had Liberty Ships named after them included Mary Cassatt, Grant Wood, and James McNeil Whistler. Writers and poets were very well represented with ships named for Edgar Allen Poe, F. Scott Fitzgerald, Joyce Kilmer, Louisa May Alcott, Mark Twain, O. Henry, Ring Lardner, Sherwood Anderson and Zane Grey.

The SS Carlos Carillo Liberty Ship, in San Francisco Bay, 1945
(Photo courtesy of U.S. Naval Historical Center)

Eighteen Liberty Ships were named after prominent African Americans, including two that were manned by all black crews. These ships included the *SS Frederick Douglass*, the *SS George Washington Carver*, the *SS Harriet Tubman* and the *SS Booker T. Washington*. Several ships were named after Native Americans including Pocahontas, Sacagawea, Chief Joseph and Tecumseh. Some of the more unusual choices for ship names were the *SS Abner Doubleday* (credited with the invention of baseball), *the SS George Gipp* ("Win one for the Gipper"), the *SS Johnny Appleseed*, and the *SS P.T. Barnum*. Perhaps the most unusual Liberty Ship moniker of all was the *SS Stage Door Canteen*. This ship was named after the well-known New York nightclub where Hollywood's greatest stars and other celebrities frequently filled in as waiters and waitresses for the visiting ordinary servicemen.

The SS Norman O. Pedrick Liberty Ship. This ship was later transferred to the U.S. Navy where it was renamed the USS Stag (Photo courtesy of U.S. Naval Historical Center)

Liberty Ships could be fitted to carry anything from tanks and Jeeps to mules. In all, about twenty-three British and American-flagged Liberty Ships were refurbished for the purpose of carrying mules to the China-Burma-India Theater. This was no easy feat. In order to transport the mules, individual stanchions had to be built for each animal, and the ships had to carry enough hay, grain and water to keep the mules alive and healthy during the trip.

Ken Laabs, who traveled to Calcutta aboard the Liberty Ship *SS W.S. Halstead*, recalled that there was one duty that was unique to the men who were on ships transporting mules. This chore had to do with the rather large amount of manure produced by the army mules. Apparently, the animal wastes were hosed down often, and then flushed out the distinctive scupper holes on the sides of the ships just above the water line. Occasionally, one of the scupper holes would become blocked, and some unfortunate soul would be sent over the side in a bosun's chair to clean it out (Laabs, pg. 10). At such times as these, it may be helpful to remember that every task, no matter how small or distasteful, worked together to secure our freedom.

The California Shipbuilding Company built the *SS Peter Silvester* as hull #0288 at Terminal Island, California. The ship's namesake was an eighteenth-century New York native who served as a representative in the First and Second Provincial Congresses as well as the First and Second Congresses of the United States.

The *Peter Silvester* had been launched for the first time on May 27, 1942, and made several safe ocean crossings before Ray Laenen had ever boarded the ship. The mission this time was simple: to deliver 317 mules from the United States to Calcutta, India where the mules would be used by troops along the Ledo and Burma Roads and on into the few areas of China which were still under Japanese control. Where Ken Laabs' Liberty Ship had undertaken a similar mission in July 1944 by following a more direct route from New Orleans, Louisiana across the Atlantic, and through the Suez Canal to Calcutta, it was no longer possible to take that route. The Peter Silvester would have to take a longer and more dangerous route, a route that would teach them firsthand about the true cost of freedom.

*Photo of a dock in Calcutta, India,
taken from the deck of a Liberty Ship.
(Photo courtesy of Library of Congress)*

Chapter Six

The Last Voyage of the
SS Peter Silvester

*To the Liberty Ship SS Peter Silvester fell the dubious
privilege of being the last Allied ship to be sunk by
enemy action in the Indian Ocean.*
- David Stevens, Australian Naval Historian

On December 31, 1944, the New Year held much promise for the Allies. The D-Day invasion of Normandy had gradually pushed the Germans back into their motherland, and the Allies had successfully repelled the Nazis' last gasp effort at Bastogne. Germany was now firmly wedged in the Allied pincer created by Russia's advance from the east, and the American advance from the west. The war in Europe was facing an inevitable conclusion, but it was not over yet. Neither the Germans nor the Japanese were ready to throw in the towel on this, the eve of 1945. In order to end the war once and for all, the Allies would need to continue feeding the supply of troops and war materiel to the front lines.

The *SS Peter Silvester* left port from Wilmington, California on December 31, 1944 under the command of Captain Bernard C. Dennis. The ship was staffed with a contingent of 174 men, including 106 U.S. Army, 26 U.S. Navy Armed Guard, and 42 Merchant Marine personnel. The U.S. Army contingent included Pvt. Ray Laenen, Tom Tschirhart, Chuck Briley and the other cavalry soldiers who were escorting the 317 mules. By a strange quirk of fate, *all* of the U.S.Army Air Force personnel who were aboard, had last names beginning with the letter H (Stevens, pg. 187). The Merchant Marines were under the employ of the ship's owner, the Pacific Far East Lines.

All of these airmen have last names beginning with the letter "H."

The first leg of the trip was uneventful. Other than a small storm or two and the jitters of a first mission, the men were in good spirits. The *Peter Silvester* made its way across the Pacific Ocean and arrived in Melbourne, Australia, on January 26th 1945. When they crossed the equator, each of the cavalrymen received a proper initiation. More seasoned sailors of the Armed Guard shaved the soldiers' heads with the clippers heretofore reserved for grooming the mules! Ship and crew made a two-night layover in Melbourne for refueling, and embarked for Colombo, Ceylon, on the morning of January 28th. Ray Laenen remembers the trip from Melbourne to the southern bight of Australia to be a pleasant one. Being so close to the equator, the weather was temperate and the companionship equally pleasant.

Space was well rationed on the Liberty Ship, although it could be argued that the mules were given more space than the men. Metal bunks were stacked four high and head to toe in the sleeping quarters. The five men from Michigan somehow managed to remain together on the ship as they had on land. In fact, one column of bunks in the second hold held Ray Laenen on the top, Tom Spicketts directly beneath him and Tom Morawski at the bottom. Tom Tschirhart and Chuck Briley were within ear shot in nearby bunks.

Each man aboard ship had his own assigned duties. The cavalrymen generally had responsibilities for the mules and other below-deck activities. The men of the Naval Armed Guard were responsible for maintaining and, if need be, firing the guns on deck. They were essentially responsible for anything to do with the defense of the ship.

All of the men were well trained for emergencies. In the event of a call to battle stations, the Armed Guard would report to their gun stations and the others would typically report to stations near the lifeboats. This was to ensure an orderly evacuation of the ship should that ever become necessary.

The SS Peter Silvester at sea

The *SS Peter Silvester* left the southeastern tip of Australia on January 28th, and steamed out into the Indian Ocean with a cargo of mules and a crew of 174 men. They would head northwest to Colombo, Ceylon (now Sri Lanka) and then ultimately to Calcutta, India. Ray Laenen recalls that the voyage was "soothing" and the men busied themselves with card games, letter writing and other means of passing time. Some constructed homemade rings out of the Australian coins they had picked up in Melbourne. Tom Tschirhart was an especially avid card player, who spent most nights up top, playing poker on deck with the men of the Armed Guard. The massive hatch covers were relatively flat, and provided the most convenient spot for the nightly card games.

Travel by sea was always wrought with danger during the war, but by all accounts the risks appeared relatively small for this mission. Over the course of the war, the Germans had sent more than a thousand U-boats into the far oceans of the world. The Indian Ocean was considered to be a low priority for both Axis and Allied forces at that time. Most of the battle action now took place on European soil and in the Pacific Ocean. Still, in February of 1945 the Japanese were far from defeated, and the Germans, with the end in sight, would try to eke out small victories wherever they could. A cornered animal can be especially dangerous. Aboard the *SS Peter Silvester*, there were rumors that a German U-boat had been sighted in the area, but since no one had actually seen one, these remained only rumors.

All things considered, this was not a good time for the German U-boats. The now infamous Enigma code had long since been broken, and Allied forces could virtually track the movement of all German U-boats as easily as their own. This intelligence victory naturally resulted in a serious reduction in the number of available German submarines. The boats that remained, were allocated primarily to the Atlantic and Pacific theaters of operation, where they could engage in battle with the strong fleet of Allied warships, and perhaps in the process, try to sink some of the Liberty Ships which now ran across the Atlantic in heavily defended convoys. Three U-boats however, were diverted to the Indian Ocean where it was known that the Allied supply ships were very busy, and often sailed without escort. Even so, the U-boat traffic in the Indian Ocean was so sparse, that at the time that the *SS Peter Silvester* sailed from Melbourne, it had been three months since a U-boat had attacked an Allied ship in the Indian Ocean (Stevens, pg. 186).

U-862 at sea circa 1945

Besatzung von U-862 im September 1944 in Singapur

Crew of the U-862

Allied submarines sank two of the U-boats that were sent to the Indian Ocean. Only the third boat remained, the *U-862*. The *U-862* was a newer, long-range German submarine, commanded by an experienced U-boat veteran, *Korvettenkapitän* Heinrich Timm. It was Timm's mission to interrupt the steady flow of Allied supplies across the Indian Ocean. So far, Timm and his crew had been very successful. In two patrols since it was put into action in July 1944, the *U-862* had been credited with the sinking of six merchant vessels (Stevens pg. 225-228). Now, however, things were relatively quiet. So quiet, in fact, for the crew of the *U-862*, that they had to find ways to relieve the boredom of days at sea with nothing to do. David Stevens reports that the crewmen took to playing silly games to entertain themselves. At one point, the men aboard the *U-862* spoke only in rhymes for days at a time. They would soon, however, be called back into action.

Captain Heinrich Timm of the U-862

For the men aboard the *Silvester*, the morning of February 6, 1945 was the start of another beautiful day at sea, at least as regards the weather. Ray Laenen remembers it to be a sunny day with calm seas. The navigator always posted a daily map so that the men would have a rough idea where they were each day. The ship was slow, making only about eight or nine knots per hour. On this day, they were about eight hundred to a thousand miles west of Australia. With eight days behind them, it would be close to a month before they would reach Calcutta.

The men went about their normal business, and in the early evening settled in to their usual free time activities. At around 9:30 PM, with the ship now about 800 miles west of Australia, Ray and his Michigan friends retired to their sleeping quarters. As they headed toward their bunks, Chuck Briley waved his friends off.

"You guys go on ahead," he said, "I'm gonna take a shower." Ray hesitated. He thought about how good a shower might feel after a long hot day, but he was tired, and decided to skip it. As Briley turned right toward the showers, Ray and the other men headed left toward the bunks. At the same time, for reasons one can only guess at later, Tom Tschirhart chose to forgo his nightly poker game with the Armed Guard soldiers on deck. Both Ray Laenen and Tom Tschirhart would later look back on those two simple decisions as the work of divine providence.

There are events in the life of every person that are so extraordinary, that a detailed image of where we were, and what we were doing at the time of the event is forever etched in our minds. All who were alive in November 1963 will remember exactly where they were when they heard that President Kennedy had been assassinated. Younger people will remember how and where they learned of the September 11, 2001 attacks on the World Trade Center and the Pentagon. Psychologists refer to these moments as "flashbulb memories" and the vivid recollections often include the most trivial of details. Ray Laenen was about to have an experience that he would remember for the rest of his life.

At 9:40 PM on the evening of February 6, 1945, two torpedoes fired from the bow of the *U-862* rammed into the starboard side of the *SS Peter Silvester*. Ray Laenen recalls that at the moment of impact, he was lying in his upper bunk reading a poem about mess kits. It was a silly, otherwise forgettable, poem about what happens to food that has been dished out into mess kits from the chow line. And yet, the simple memory of that moment would live with Ray forever.

The two torpedoes struck the hull of the ship so close together, that many at first thought it had only been one torpedo. The powerful explosion blew the massive iron hatchcovers hundreds of feet into the air, instantly killing the men of the Armed Guard who sat atop them playing poker. Despite having lookouts for just such a possibility, no one on the ship saw or heard the torpedoes before they struck. One can only guess that at the moment of their deaths, the men were perhaps thinking only of what card to play next. That night, Tom Tschirhart was dealt a lucky hand.

The violent explosion immediately cut all power and light within the vessel. Flying shrapnel severed the radio antennas as if they were twigs. On the top bunk, a metal ventilation duct broke loose from its moorings and crashed down heavily on the bridge of Ray Laenen's nose. He was thrown from his bunk down onto the bulkhead of the ship. Later, he would thank God that he hadn't been knocked unconscious at that moment. If he had, he might not have been here to tell the story. Bleeding and in total darkness, Ray cried out for his bunkmates.

"Spicketts! Morawski! Where are you?" he called.

The men somehow found each other and groped their way through the darkness and oily smelling dust to the spot where, only moments before, a staircase to the deck had been. It was no longer there. They found instead, a metal ladder, which had been built behind the staircase, perhaps as a backup for just such an emergency, perhaps just some leftover detritus of the construction process.

Laenen and Morawski were ambulatory, but Spicketts was hurt badly, and could not make it up the ladder by himself. His leg had been shattered, and was bleeding profusely. Together, Ray and Tom Morawski, numbed yet energized by adrenaline, carried the injured Spicketts up the ladder to the chaotic, but presumably safer deck. Once up top, the men reported to their battle stations, and frantically planned for the possible evacuation of the vessel.

Nearby, closer to the point of impact, steel girders were twisted like pipe cleaners, and coated with heavy machine oil. Seawater rushed in to fill the void where, seconds before, men had worked. Private Jim Clark tried to escape the horrific chaos but could not get a grip on the slippery steel. At one point, the wooden deck gave way beneath him and he nearly fell into the hold, saved only by the metal crosspiece he had grabbed on his way down.

Chuck Kemmer liked to use his life preserver as a pillow. He had just climbed into his bunk about fifteen minutes earlier. When the first torpedo hit, Kemmer, like Ray, was knocked out of his bunk on to the hard steel floor. After he hit the deck, he tried to find the life preserver, feeling that somehow, he might need it soon. He blindly swept his arm around in the pungent darkness but never did find the life preserver.

The location of the first hit was, from the point of view of U-boat Captain Timm, almost perfect. The torpedoes smashed into the starboard side of the *SS Peter Silvester*, just in front of the bridge and roughly at the front of the second cargo hold. The concussion had literally torn the ship in half, with the bow section seeming to be in almost immediate danger of sinking. The stern section looked very questionable, and could not be far behind. The Germans expected the ship to sink quickly. One crewmember of the *U-862* wrote with glee in his diary that day that they were pleased to have stumbled across another *Kaisersarg*, which roughly translates into "Kaiser coffin," the Germans' derogatory name for the Liberty Ships.

Ray and most of his Michigan shipmates had been in hold number three directly behind the point of impact, which gave them very little time to take care of business. Chuck Briley, who had decided to take a shower before bed, was killed instantly. Ray would later wish that he could once more hear his friend pine away for his sweet Marie.

In the partial moonlight, the men could see just enough on deck to know what they were doing. They stumbled toward their battle stations at the lifeboats. Although one might expect there to be massive confusion at such a time, Ray remembered the scenario to be relatively orderly. He attributes this lack of panic to the professionalism of the men and the fact that they had trained incessantly for just such an occasion.

The initial explosion had blown several of the lifeboats off the ship. For those not lucky enough to make it to one of the four remaining lifeboats, there were large six crude wooden rafts.

The *SS Peter Silvester* turned out to be much sturdier than many of the Liberty Ship naysayers had predicted. Thirty minutes after breaking in half, both sections of the ship remained afloat. This fact was not lost on the German U-boat Commander, who then ordered two more torpedoes fired into the stricken ship's hull. In an almost prescient act, after the first torpedoes hit, Captain Dennis told the men to expect more. About thirty to forty minutes after the first explosion, two more torpedoes smashed into the starboard side at about the same location as the first two.

Don Tuthill had been knocked out of his bunk after the first round of torpedoes. When the second round exploded, he was catapulted through the air and landed on some sharp oily steel one or two decks below. Ocean water was rushing in all around him and he knew that he needed to get out of there fast. He had several cuts and contusions from the fall and heard another man loudly reciting the *Lord's Prayer*. Tuthill made it up to the top deck when the final round of torpedoes struck. Again he was knocked off of his feet, and thrown across the deck. He believes that he was the last man in that part of the ship to make it out alive.

After that second round of torpedoes exploded, Captain Dennis gave the order to abandon ship. With all of the electricity knocked out, he issued his order through the horn of a megaphone. Ray and the remaining cavalrymen assisted in the evacuation to the lifeboats.

One of the lifeboats was reserved for the injured. Ray Laenen and Tom Morawski helped their friend Tom Spicketts to the boat, but Spicketts protested that he wanted to stay with his friends. Laenen and Morawski knew that this lifeboat would also contain Captain Dennis and a veterinarian. The veterinarian was on board to care for the mules, but now he would be of more value to the injured men. Ray and Tom Tschirhart insisted that Spicketts get into the lifeboat that contained the essential medical resources. Ultimately, he relented. He agreed to separate from his friends and was lowered into the lifeboat. Spicketts later would remember Captain Dennis to be a very fine man who saved many men that night.

With most of the other men already evacuated, Laenen, and Morawski lowered themselves into a remaining lifeboat. The ship was heaving and thrashing about like a wounded whale as metal ladders and nets crashed heavily against the hull. With no other choice, Ray and Tom hung on for dear life, and climbed down to the lifeboat.

As they entered the boat, they realized that someone had left the petcock open and the lifeboat was rapidly sinking. It was nearly submerged and still tethered to the sinking *SS Peter Silvester*. They briefly considered whether they should close the petcock and attempt to bail the boat out, but feared that the lifeboat would be sucked down with the ship before they could render it seaworthy. Ray vividly remembered films from his training, that showed that a sinking ship would create a water vacuum and pull anybody or anything that was nearby, down with the ship. There was no time to waste. Tom and

Ray jumped into the dark, oily sea and swam through debris toward the dim, bobbing lights of another lifeboat that floated about fifty yards from the sinking ship.

It would be hard to imagine a more terrifying swim. In the darkness, Ray kept his eyes on the dancing lights as he swam toward the other lifeboat. He nearly choked on the thick oil that floated in globs on the surface of the otherwise placid Indian Ocean. As he swam, he passed other men in the water, some alive, some not. Amidst the flotsam, Ray threaded his way through a gantlet of frantic, thrashing mules. Some mules had already drowned, while others tried furiously to tread water. The plaintive screams of the dying mules echoed through the night, the dreadful sound deeply scarring another dark place in Ray Laenen's memory.

When Ray reached the other lifeboat, he found it packed with more than thirty men. A second boat, containing only a few men, was partially submerged and tethered by rope to the first boat. It also looked to be in danger of sinking. Ray was helped into the more crowded boat, safe at last for the time being. As he entered the boat, he was relieved to see the face of his good friend Tom Tschirhart, already aboard. Amazingly, Tom Morawski soon climbed into the same boat.

Meanwhile, Don Tuthill and Chuck Kemmer swam through the muck and tried to enter the same lifeboat. At first, the men would not let Tuthill into the boat because it was already overcrowded. Don was still bleeding profusely, and feared that his own blood would attract sharks. Eventually, the men relented and allowed Tuthill to climb into the boat. Chuck Kemmer was not so lucky. He remained in the water, hanging desperately to the side of the lifeboat throughout the entire night. He was not alone. He now recalls, "There were a lot of us in the water that first night."

Some of the mules tried to climb into the lifeboats and had to be beaten off with oars and fists. If even one mule had climbed over the gunwale, it would have meant disaster for the men inside the boat. Still, it broke the hearts of these young men to watch the mules eventually give up and slip helplessly below the oil-soaked surface of the waves.

About fifteen to twenty minutes after the second round of torpedoes hit, another explosion rocked the wounded vessel. This third and last attack was the most violent, reportedly lifting the bow section clean out of the water. The official Army report of the incident suggests that this third explosion may have been caused by two more torpedoes or possibly by the deck mounted guns of the *U-862*. In either case, the damage was done, and the bow section of the *SS Peter Silvester* plunged deep beneath the surface of the sea.

As the men huddled together in the lifeboat, Ray Laenen didn't know what would happen next. He watched the ship on which he had sailed from America, now slowly sinking below the surface of the ocean. Still, he didn't give up hope. Ray was a natural optimist, a glass-half-full type of guy. In addition, his strong Catholic faith helped him to believe that somehow, some way, he would get out of this alive. He touched the small scapular medal that hung next to his dogtags. In the minutes and weeks to come, Ray's faith and optimism would be tested, but would never fail.

The first test came about ninety minutes after that last round of torpedoes. Having survived a U-boat attack, and having witnessed the destruction of their ship, the men took some comfort in the fact that they were at least alive and in a lifeboat. Whatever solace they may have taken at that point was soon shattered by the sound of the diesel engines of the *U-862*. The German U-boat, after confirming its kill, had surfaced no more than twenty feet from Ray's lifeboat, to survey the damage. Its periscope punched up through the surface of the water like a cobra searching for prey. The sound of the engines projected an ominous cadence - *chug-chug-chug,* as its searchlight scanned the waters to see what damage it had done.

Captain Timm (left) on deck of U-862

At that moment, Ray had some fleeting doubts. He had seen Allied propaganda movies during his training, which showed that German U-boats would often surface after an attack, strafe the area and kill any survivors. He peered over the gunwale of the boat and thought, "My God, here I am, eighteen years old. I'm thinking of my mother, my father, my brother… and I thought 'this is going to be the last day of my life." It was not.

Captain Timm never gave the order to fire on the survivors. Why not? For the most part, the idea of German U-boat crews killing survivors was a myth (Hewittson). It can be assumed that a professional U-boat captain, once having achieved his objective in the sinking of a ship, has no interest in slaughtering survivors. Also, one must consider that a submarine is most vulnerable when it is on the surface of the water, and so will minimize this vulnerability by remaining underwater as much as possible. Unfortunately, there *were* many documented incidents of Japanese submarines killing survivors. Japanese Rear Admiral Mito Hisashi issued the following order to the 1st Japanese Submarine Force in 1943:

> *"All submarines will act together in order to concentrate their attacks against enemy convoys and totally destroy them. Do not stop with the sinking of enemy ships and cargoes; at the same time carry out the complete destruction of the crews of the enemy ships; if possible, seize the crew and endeavor to secure information about the enemy* (Elphick, pg. 359)

It may have been another of the many life saving coincidences to which Ray attributes his survival, that this particular submarine was German and not Japanese. Ray and the other men in the lifeboats breathed deep sighs of relief when the U-boat finally slipped silently beneath the waves.

Although one might be hard-pressed to consider oneself lucky after having your ship sunk by a German torpedo, Ray Laenen considered himself just that. His religious faith and eternal optimism allowed him to see the positive in a situation that could otherwise only be described as tragic. Thirty-two men aboard the *SS Peter Silvester* were not so lucky that night. They were killed either in the initial explosions, or in the resulting attempts to seek refuge in one of the lifeboats or rafts. The remaining 142 men were able to make it to one of the four lifeboats or six life rafts. For those men, the worst was yet to come.

Chapter Seven

Lost at Sea

The miserable have no other medicine
But only hope.
– William Shakespeare,
(from *All's Well That Ends Well*)

o one slept that night. Ray Laenen's lifeboat was packed with thirty men who wore their fear, anger and sadness like tragic masks on tattered bodies. Many of the men, who had been in their bunks at the time of the attack, were still in their underwear. When the sun came up over the Indian Ocean, Ray could see in the far off distance that the stern section of the *SS Peter Silvester* was still partially afloat. This fact surprised not only the men in the lifeboat, but Captain Timm of the *U-862* as well. What Ray and the other men did not know, was that the night before, when the U-boat had surfaced, Captain Timm considered boarding the stricken vessel to see what kind of secret cargo the ship contained. He, like most U-boat captains, has been told that the Liberty Ships were so poorly built that they would sink immediately when hit. He surmised that the *Peter Silvester*, because it did not sink after multiple torpedo hits, must have been carrying some special cargo. It is a pity that he did not board the ship, because it would have been a great surprise for him to inspect the "special cargo" of mules and their hay.

Albert Schirrmann (left front) and U-862 crewmembers getting fresh air

In the daylight, it became apparent that some rearrangement was in order. First, Captain Dennis took a small search party back on to the stricken hull to retrieve a supply of food, water and warm clothing. As they returned, the purser tossed the men some shirts, sweaters and pants. Ray was thrown a pair of blue trousers that were several sizes too small, and so tight he couldn't close them all the way. At that time, he had an athletic build and weighed over 190 pounds. Thankful for anything, he pulled the pants up as far as he could and counted his blessings.

Next, they would need to reassign some of the lifeboats' occupants. Thirty men were crowded into Ray's lifeboat, while the flooded boat, still tethered to the first, held only two or three. One of the men in the second boat had died of his injuries during the night, and was given a makeshift burial at sea.

There were two officers aboard Ray's lifeboat. Captain Charles Hatfield of the U.S. Army Transportation Corps was responsible for overseeing the transport of mules and Army personnel to Burma. He had no responsibility for the operation of the ship itself, or its lifeboats. Luckily, Jack Easley, the second mate of the *SS Peter Silvester* was also aboard. As the ranking officer (and ironically, the son-in-law of Captain Dennis), Easley immediately took charge of the lifeboat and its crew. He ordered the men to bail the second boat out, and began to assign several men to transfer from the crowded boat to the near-empty boat.

Chuck Kemmer, still clinging to the side of a lifeboat was finally allowed to climb out of the sea and into the newly bailed boat.

At that point, Ray and Tom Tschirhart were still together. Chuck Briley had been killed in the initial explosion and Tom Spicketts was in a different lifeboat with Captain Dennis, but Ray, Tom Tschirhart, Don Tuthill and Tom Morawski remained together in the crowded boat. One by one, 2nd Mate Easley ordered some men to move to the other boat. When Tom Tschirhart was ordered to move, Ray tried to join him.

"Wait a minute," said Easley, "that's enough."

Ray tried to plead his case to the 2nd Mate.

"But that's my friend Tom," he begged.

Easley held his ground.

"That's enough," he repeated, "Laenen, you stay here."

Jack Easley was only interested in balancing the load of each boat, not preserving friendships. Ray was crestfallen. He had already lost his friend Chuck Briley, and seen Tom Spicketts suffer serious injury. Now he was separated from his best friend, and neither knew if they would see each other again. To make matters worse, Tom's boat had to be cut loose from Ray's boat. It was too difficult to maneuver the cumbersome craft together, and Easley made the decision to separate them. That way, the lighter second boat might be able to make its way back to Australia first and expedite the rescue of the other.

The boats drifted apart and slowly went their own ways. The other boat, now containing both Tom Tschirhart and Chuck Kemmer proved to be a little bit faster. The men in the faster boat said that they would sail for a while and then wait for the other boat to catch up. By sundown that evening, the two boats were so far apart, that the men could no longer see each other. It was the last they would see of each other for quite some time.

Only 2nd Mate Easley knew how far from shore the men really were. In order to keep up morale, Easley lied to the men. He told them that they were only 200 miles from shore, and could easily make it back to land. Easley's little falsehood allowed the men to feel sure that they would be picked up or rescued very soon. Easley, of course, knew differently. He knew that they were actually more than 800 miles west of Australia, and that the likelihood of rescue decreased with every day that they were not found. To his credit, he kept that information to himself.

Ray Laenen (smiling in center) and Tom Morawski (to right of Ray) in lifeboat

The lifeboat was twenty-six feet long and perhaps ten feet wide. It was made of sturdy wood and had a red canvas sail (for visibility from afar), a tiller, and a built-in compass. There were air tanks built-in under the seats to improve buoyancy. Still, with twenty men aboard, and a hull shaped like a fisherman's skiff, it was no America's Cup contender. The men watched the compass, and tried their best to keep the boat headed due east. Each man took his turn at tiller duty. They sat shoulder to shoulder in the small boat and moved counter-clockwise every two hours to the next position. With no sextant or other navigational aids, this was the best that they could do. Head east. Head east.

Aboard the lifeboat, the men had little to drink and even less to eat. Water rationing began on the first day. The water supply came in small sealed cans. Each man was allowed to drink a little less than one pint per day. Again, this is where the good army training paid off. At first glance, it appeared that they had plenty of water, but that assessment was based on the assumption that they would be rescued within a few days. Had that been the case, the men could have consumed almost as much water each day as they wanted. Second Mate Easley, however, based his allocation on the *minimum* amount needed to keep the men alive. He knew that a small lifeboat in an area the size of the Indian Ocean would be difficult to find even in the best of circumstances. And because the power had been knocked out immediately when the torpedoes hit meant that no SOS signal had been sent. It could be days or weeks before anyone even realized that the *Peter Silvester* was missing. This being the case, Easley could not risk the water supply (or the lives of his men) on an overly optimistic estimate of how long they would be adrift. His decision to ration the water conservatively was wise, if not prescient.

For food, the men had only small cans of pemmican, a little bit of chocolate, some hard crackers and a few days worth of malted milk tablets. Some of the crackers were ruined when the wax seals on the packages cracked and let moisture in. The pemmican was a lifesaver. Pemmican is a concentrated mixture of dried fish, fruit, coconut, suet, and other high protein ingredients, that is made primarily for two purposes – to provide the most sustenance in the smallest possible package, and to last a long time without refrigeration. It is believed to have been invented by North American Indians, and was used for food in winter months and at times when other food sources would not be readily available. Pound for pound, pemmican provides much more nutrition than almost any other food, and has been making a comeback of sorts in the twenty-first century among hikers, hunters and natural food aficionados. The supply of pemmican was also carefully rationed, with each man having about ¼ can (each about the size of a tuna fish can) three times per day.

Sleep was accomplished by way of each man hanging his head down toward his lap. You couldn't lean back for fear of falling out of the boat, and there was no room to lie down. Still, somehow they slept. Some slept out of exhaustion, others to avoid thinking about the reality of their situation.

The men aboard Ray's lifeboat coped with their situation in different ways. At first, they talked about anything to remind them of life back home. They talked of the things they missed: baseball, beer, and pretty women. They wondered aloud about their comrades who were not on that lifeboat. Who made it out alive, and who didn't, they wondered? Food was a common topic for the first week or so. The men would take turns describing their favorite dish or dessert, only to laugh at the ridiculousness of the current diet. "Man!" one guy would say, "I could go for a big juicy *Wimpy's* hamburger right now, with lettuce and tomatoes and the works." Another would yearn for a *Sanders* hot fudge sundae or a tall cool glass of *Stroh's* beer. Such talk helped the men to try and minimize the seriousness of their situation, much like a man whistling as he walks past the graveyard at midnight.

The food banter died out when the men stopped feeling hungry. Their stomachs had shrunk, and they no longer felt such an urge to eat. They also no longer saw the humor in describing meals that they might never eat again.

The boat was supplied with one almost comically small fishing rod, and an artificial lure with which a few of the men managed to catch just one tiny fish. Rather than eat the small fish, the men decided that they would cut it into pieces that they would then use as bait to catch bigger fish. They cut the fish up and put the pieces into a can to be used the next day. When they awoke the next morning, they discovered that the can was empty. Weeks later, one of the men, a Merchant Marine, admitted that he had become so hungry that he ate the fish while the others were asleep. The next day they lost the hook, as well as their hope for catching any more fish.

The men on Tom Tschirhart's boat also tried unsuccessfully to catch a fish. Chuck Kemmer recalls that they fashioned a crude net from strips of wood which they had peeled off of the seats. When they put the net into the water the wood swelled up and absorbed so much seawater that they feared it would drag the boat down with it. They also abandoned their hopes of having a fresh fish dinner.

On February 10th, Don Tuthill "celebrated" his nineteenth birthday. There were no presents and no cake for the young man. Later he would tease his comrades about their lack of sensitivity in ignoring his birthday.

After a week or two, the men ran out of things to talk about, and for the remainder of the time did not speak much at all. The men turned inward, some to their own thoughts and fears, others to God. Ray was in the latter group. He treasured his Catholic faith and frequently touched the medal next to his dogtag. He prayed silently but every day, never losing hope that he and his friends would be rescued. "I never lost faith," he said. "I knew that we would be picked up." For this, credit should be given both to Ray's religious faith and to his naturally sunny disposition. One photograph, taken aboard the lifeboat by the ship's radioman early in the ordeal, seems to show Ray Laenen as the only man in the boat with any expression even remotely resembling a smile.

Not everyone on board was as optimistic as Ray Laenen was. Many of the men, including Tom Morawski, slipped into a deep sense of helpless depression. Ray recalls that Morawski remained very serious throughout the ordeal and "never smiled or cracked a joke the whole time." By the second week, many had given up any hope that they would be found. Depression filled the void where hope used to be. Ray tried his best to encourage those who had lost hope, but there was not much he could do to change their outlook. After all, Ray's optimism was based on a level of faith and strength of character that not many others could match.

After seven days at sea, someone in the boat spotted what appeared to be an airplane far off in the distance. They shot off a flare, but the plane did not see it, and disappeared into the horizon. They later learned that it was an Allied aircraft which, while missing Ray's boat, did find one of the six crude liferafts from the *SS Peter Silvester*. All of the men aboard that raft were safely rescued.

Liferafts tethered together at point of rescue

A raft is rescued by the USS Corpus Christi

A raft is rescued by the USS Corpus Christi

The rescue effort for the *SS Peter Silvester* began about four days after the sinking, when a merchant vessel serendipitously came across one of the lifeboats. Prior to that, no one even knew that the ship was missing, let alone sunk. That first lifeboat sighting initiated one of the largest search and rescue operations of the war. "At one stage it involved virtually every Allied warship or merchant ship in the eastern Indian Ocean (Stevens, 192)." Clearly, there were a lot of people in the air and sea looking for Ray Laenen and his shipwrecked mates.

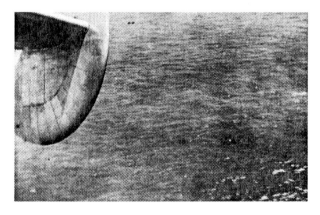

Needle in a haystack – two rafts (upper left) are sighted by an Australian B-24 Liberator during massive airsearch

The men began to get testy with one another due to the close quarters. Ray's boat was so crowded that it was impossible for any one person to lie down. The men sat shoulder to shoulder for two hours at a time, with their feet submerged under four to six inches of salty bilge water. Many developed a malady called "immersion foot," which, depending on the severity, led to lifelong problems in some cases. Don Tuthill recalls that "My feet hurt so bad by the time we were picked up, that I couldn't stand it."

When shift change was announced for the tiller duty, each man would gingerly crawl to the next spot without standing or otherwise jeopardizing the safety of the others. At times, arguments would erupt and one man would yell at another for no crime other than the fact that their bodies were touching. Ray managed to keep his temper under control, but he recalled many of the other guys often saying things like, "Get the hell off of me for crying out loud!" Second Mate Easley allowed the men to blow off a certain amount of steam, but there were no physical altercations. By maintaining military order and discipline, Easley and Hatfield were able to keep the situation from deteriorating into a *Lord of the Flies* type scenario.

On about the twelfth to fifteenth day, the boredom and lethargy of the men was broken up by yet another threat to their safety. As they stared into the endless ocean waves, they saw a large pod of whales swimming around, and at times underneath, the lifeboat. This was quite unnerving, as the large creatures could have easily overturned the small boat with one quick flick of a fluke. Many people now pay good money to go on whale watching expeditions, but for the men in that small lifeboat, it was a terrifying ordeal. Ray said another prayer, and recalls that within a few minutes "the whales went off on their merry way." Before they left, Ray had a recurrence of the fear that he had experienced when the *U-862* had surfaced before his eyes. "Wouldn't this be ironic," he thought, "after all of this, to die because of being overturned by a school of whales!"

For the most part, the weather protected the survivors. The sky remained cloudy most of the time, and for that reason the men did not suffer any serious sunburn. Ironically, when the sun did come out, the men were somewhat protected by the thick coat of dirty oil that covered much of their exposed skin. Also, being so close to the equator, it did not get too cold at night. There were storms, however. When it rained, the men tried to capture as much fresh water as possible in their mouths, hats and other clothing.

On a couple of occasions, the small lifeboat had to ride the crests and valleys of monstrous ocean waves. Ray remembers the worst storm occurring on a Sunday, about twenty days after the sinking. There were roiling waves of thirty to forty feet. It was like being on a giant open elevator that rose and fell without anyone having the slightest bit of control over it.

"We thought we were going to die when the boat slammed down to the bottom of those waves," said Ray. Despite the battering, the boat held up. Ray marveled at how well the boats held together under such stress. The men did not necessarily hold up as well.

The food supply was gone before the second week was completed. It almost didn't matter. The rations had been so small that their stomachs had grown used to very little food intake. By the third week, some of the men were beginning to hallucinate. They would look out into the empty horizon and proclaim that they could see a lighthouse, or a ship or an airplane. Others who were still lucid would tell them to shut up and sit down. At such times, majority rule can often be the best anchor for one's sanity.

Early in the morning of February 28th, the twenty-second day at sea, one of the men gave Ray a tiny pocket bible. Ray doesn't remember why the man gave it to him, but he was glad to take it. He opened it randomly to the Book of Mark, and began to read:

Therefore I tell you, whatever you ask in prayer, believe that you will receive it, and you will (Mark 11; 22)

Ray had always prayed on a regular basis anyway, but this scripture seemed, to him, to be a confirmation that his many prayers were being heard. A few hours later, just before noon, Captain Hatfield thought that he saw something on the horizon. "There's a ship out there!" he yelled.

"Sure, sure" the men replied with ennui. They had heard this kind of thing many, many times before over the past few weeks, and were not about to get too excited over another man's delusions.

"I tell ya', there's a ship out there!" Hatfield repeated.

The men in the lifeboat didn't know if these were Japanese or Allied aircraft (HMS Activity)

Actually, Captain Hatfield was in the best position to see across the horizon as he was situated in the bow of the boat, farther forward than any other man. Partly because he was their captain, and partly because he was so insistent, the men began to scan the ocean for any sign of a ship. Before long, others confirmed what Hatfield had seen. This time, they were right. There *was* a ship out there.

Chapter Eight

Rescued!

He delivers and rescues, He works signs and wonders in heaven and on earth, He who has saved Daniel from the power of the lions.
– Daniel, 6.27

The ship that Captain Hatfield saw in the distance was the *HMS Activity*, a British Royal Navy escort aircraft carrier making its way from the East Indies to Sydney, Australia. Like the Liberty Ships, the Escort Carriers were built rapidly, specifically for the war effort. They were smaller than purpose-built carriers, with an improvised flight deck welded atop a hull that was previously used for standard shipping.

On that day, the ship and crew of the *Activity* were practicing evasive maneuvers for preparation in the event of expected Kamikaze attacks. The ship was equipped with a special stern controller, which allowed it to turn on a ninety-degree axis. They would zigzag left and right in a manner that would make it more difficult for a Kamikaze pilot to hit his mark. The Officer on Watch aboard the *Activity* that morning, was Lieutenant L.L.F. Sinclair, of the British Royal Naval Reserve. Scanning the waves, he thought that he spotted something in the water that could perhaps be the conning tower of a submarine. As the ship got closer to the object, Sinclair determined that it was instead a small boat with a bright red sail. The *HMS Activity* circled the object carefully, as it was known at that time that some Japanese submarines would lure unsuspecting ships into a trap, where they would be torpedoed.

In the meantime, the men aboard Ray's lifeboat did everything they could to make sure the men on the ship saw them. They sent up three parachute flares and an orange colored smoke-bomb. Captain Hatfield fired his service revolver into the air as other crewmen waved a yellow distress flag high above their heads.

As the ship drew closer, the men in the lifeboat could see bright round insignias on the sides of the airplanes atop the deck of the ship. From a distance, they mistook the bullseye insignia of the British RAF for the Rising Sun insignia of a Japanese aircraft. At that point, Ray recalled, they almost didn't care whether it was an Allied ship or a Japanese ship. They were out of food and would not last much longer adrift at sea. Captain Hatfield reassured the men that this was not an enemy ship. Relieved, Ray Laenen took the opportunity to thank God for hearing his prayers. "Thank you, Lord," was all he said.

Once the men realized that they were about to be rescued, some of them began to open cans of water and gulp freely for the first time in twenty-two days.

Photo of the rescue of Ray Laenen's lifeboat taken from the deck of the HMS Activity

In another of the many *coincidences* for which Ray Laenen is now thankful, the zigzag maneuvers of the big ship put them in the only position where they could have seen the tiny speck of a lifeboat in the ocean. If not for the evasive maneuver training, their course would not have taken them to the exact spot where the bright red sail of the lifeboat was sighted. The *HMS Activity* circled closer until the tiny craft could be seen clearly and then still closer until it was finally at the ship's side. As the two boats came together, someone aboard the *Activity* had the foresight to take photographs of the men in the boat. These snapshots would later become treasured keepsakes for the men of the *SS Peter Silvester* who were rescued that day.

The captain of the *HMS Activity* would later write that, had they not spotted the lifeboat at that moment, it most likely would never have been rescued. Apparently, the trade winds would have taken the small boat far out of the sight of any would-be rescuers.

HMS Activity from the air

As most of the men were being raised up to the deck in cargo nets, Ray Laenen, in his anticipatory excitement, couldn't wait. Not a man to leave his fate in the hands of others, Ray climbed out of the lifeboat and scurried up a rope ladder that hung over the side of the heaving aircraft carrier. He was unaware, however, of just how much of a toll the lack of food and water had taken on his body. Over the twenty-two days he was adrift, his once athletic frame had shrunk by almost fifty pounds. Those once-too-tight blue pants that had been thrown to him by the purser now hung tarp-like over his hips, several sizes too big. In addition, the only exercise Ray had had over the past three weeks was the minimal act of shuffling around to the next position in the tiller rotation.

All of the men aboard that lifeboat had unknowingly suffered significant muscle atrophy. As Ray reached the top of the ladder, he began to feel faint. Ignoring the feedback from his brain, he continued to climb regardless - and then unceremoniously passed out just as he was lifted over the rail. His twenty-two day ordeal at sea was over.

The men would not have to wait long to, once again, set foot on terra firma. Because of the rescue of these twenty men (and an emergency appendectomy by one crewmember of the *Activity*), the ship did not continue its scheduled journey to Sydney. Instead, the *HMS Activity* changed course and set anchor at the much closer Perth/Fremantle port on the West Coast of Australia. Along the way, the men were allowed to eat their first real food in more than three weeks – but not much of it. The ship's doctor knew that food would have to be introduced in small increments because that the men's stomachs had shrunk and their digestive tracts had all but shut down. They were given small bowls of soup at first, and then gradually introduced to more substantial food.

One British Seaman aboard the HMS Activity was Bob Taylor. Years later, Taylor would send a letter to Ray Laenen, thereby initiating a correspondence and friendship between these two men from different countries. The two men, to their knowledge, had never met, but they shared a common purpose and a significant moment in time.

British crewman Bob Taylor of the HMS Activity, 1945

Once in Perth, the men were admitted to the Hollywood Military Hospital. Hollywood Hospital was a five-hundred bed facility built in 1942 by the Australians to care for service personnel during the war. There were no Hollywood celebrities in this hospital, only the brave soldiers of Britain, Australia and the United States, wounded in the cause of protecting our freedoms. The hospital still exists but was privatized in 1994. The current owners have honored the history of the hospital by naming each wing for a different recipient of Australia's Victoria Cross and George Cross medals of honor.

Hollywood Hospital, Perth Australia, 1945

Ray received treatment for various scrapes, bruises and lacerations he had received to his legs when the *Peter Silvester* was sunk. The wound he had received on the bridge of his nose was the least of his concerns, as it was healing on its own. Of more pressing concern was the need to gain back his weight and strength, and to treat the case of immersion foot that he developed – as with all of his shipmates. Vitamins, exercise and protein enriched food were the order of the day.

Ray's first concern while at the hospital was not himself. It was the welfare of his other shipmates, the men who were not on his lifeboat. He especially worried about his best friend Tom Tschirhart.

Ray felt disheartened to think that he and Tom had remained together through everything, only to be separated at the last moment. Now, Tom Tschirhart's boat was the only one that had not been rescued. He checked with the hospital staff each day.

"Who was picked up?" he asked, "Who survived?"

The answer to his questions would provide some relief but more cause for concern. He found out first that all but one of the lifeboats and rafts had already been picked up. His friend Tom Spicketts with the wounded leg was already in Perth. In fact, in the weeks between the time Spicketts was rescued and the time Ray was rescued, Spicketts had already been discharged from the same hospital! With more than a two-week head start on Ray, Tom was on the mend and getting better each day. His was the first boat to be rescued, two days after the sinking. Given the condition of his leg, one can only wonder whether he would have survived if he were not in the first boat rescued.

Spicketts and fourteen other survivors had been picked up on February 8, 1945, by the *SS Cape Edmont,* which was sailing from Calcutta to Melbourne, Australia, with a cargo of used army aircraft motors. It was somewhat ironic that this ship was returning on the same route that the *SS Peter Silvester* would have taken had it completed its mission.

Less than a week after Tom Spickett's lifeboat was rescued, the *USS Corpus Christi*, a patrol frigate, had picked up another sixty-two survivors. In contrast to the lifeboat that held Ray Laenen and his shipmates, some of the other boats and rafts had managed to stick closer together. The *Corpus Christi* had rescued sixty-two men at the same time from one lifeboat and six rafts. The rafts had been tethered together. Without sails, there was no reason for them to sever the ropes that bound them to each other.

The USS Corpus Christi

One day, Tom Spicketts was told that Ray and the other men in his boat had been picked up. Tom went to the hospital, but could barely recognize his friend Ray. Tom recalls that "Ray had lost so much weight, and he had blisters all over his legs from exposure to the salt water." Regardless, the two men were glad to renew their acquaintance under any circumstances.

With the rescue of the men from Ray Laenen's lifeboat, that left only one boat still unaccounted for – the one that held Ray's best friend, Tom Tschirhart. It had now been almost four weeks since the *SS Peter Silvester* had perished. As each day passed, Ray would go to the hospital's front desk and ask the same question: "Have you heard any word yet about the last lifeboat?" Each day, he would get the same answer: "No, nothing."

Ray began to rehearse in his mind how he would explain to Tom's parents what had happened. He knew that Mr. and Mrs. Tschirhart would hear the news officially from the Army, but he would still have to tell them the details himself. It was a task he dreaded.

Back in Detroit, Gustaf and Josephine Laenen knew nothing of what had happened to their son. For reasons of military security, families were not routinely informed of the whereabouts of soldiers. On March 6, 1945, one month to the day after the Peter Silvester was sunk, and one day after Ray Laenen was rescued, the Laenen family received the following telegram from the U.S. Army:

> THE SECRETARY OF WAR DESIRES ME TO EXPRESS HIS DEEP REGRET THAT YOUR SON PRIVATE REMIE LAENEN HAS BEEN REPORTED MISSING IN ACTION SINCE SIX FEBRUARY IN SOUTHWEST PACIFIC AREA IF FURTHER DETAILS OR OTHER INFORMATION ARE RECEIVED YOU WILL BE PROMPTLY NOTIFIED.
> J A ULIO THE ADJUTANT GENERAL

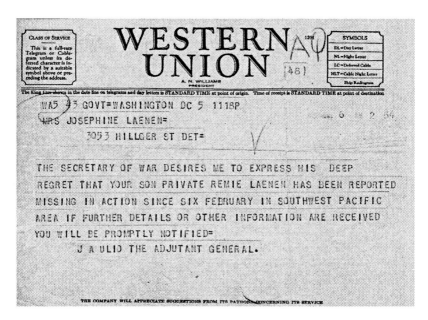

*The first telegram received by the Laenens informing
them that Ray Laenen was missing in action*

What can a parent do in response to such news? The Laenens, of course, prayed. Josephine also decided, as do many people when they bargain with God, to make a personal sacrifice. She would give up her cigarettes until her son was safely returned to her arms. By now, the smoking habit had taken full hold and was as much a part of Josephine's life as her baking and sewing. It is natural in times of crisis for a person to try to do *something* in order to feel that they have some vestige of control over the situation. Bargaining with God allows a person to feel that their behavior will, in some small way, influence the object of their prayers. Ultimately, Josephine would keep her promise for a year and a half.

The very next day, on March 7, 1945, the Laenens received a second telegram. This one, however, did not come from the army. A kind nurse at Hollywood Hospital had sent the message for Ray. It was concise:

"ALL WELL AND SAF.E LOVE REMIE LAENEN."

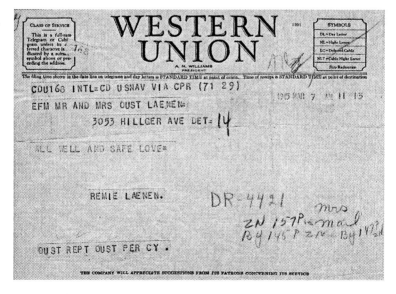

Telegram received by the Laenens the very next day

Try convincing a devout Catholic that this rapid response was anything but an answer from God. There was little rhyme or reason to the timing of the two telegrams. The first one, sent by the army was a month late. The second telegram, sent a month after the sinking, arrived one day after the first telegram. Whatever the cause for the Army's delay in sending the first telegram, the end result was that Ray's parents only lost one night of sleep wondering if their son was alive or dead. This by no means ended the worrying, but it gave Josephine and Gustaf Laenen a reason to believe that their son would return safely to them after all. Their prayers had been answered and answered quickly.

On April 7, 1945, the U.S Army finally sent its own telegram to inform the Laenens that Remie was hospitalized somewhere in the Southwest Pacific. Like the first telegram, it was a month late and gave no details on his condition. If it weren't for that Australian nurse in Perth, Ray's parents would have waited four weeks to find out that their oldest son was still alive.

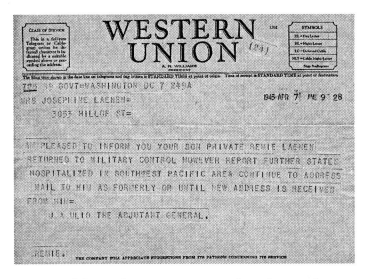

A month later, the Laenens received notification from the Army that their son was injured but alive

Back at Hollywood Hospital, Ray continued to make inquiries as to the whereabouts of Tom Tschirhart, but it was looking more and more desperate each day. The survivors of the SS *Peter Silvester* made up only a small percentage of the hospital patients. There were British, Australian and American men and women of all military services being treated at the hospital, with new arrivals every day. Such is the nature of war that the hospital beds rarely go vacant for long.

On the tenth day of Ray's recovery the man in the next bed, an Australian soldier, was discharged. After the man was gone, Ray took a long walk around the hallways and down to the lavatory. He was determined to get the exercise he needed to regain his strength. When he returned from his walk, he found that the vacant bed across from his had already been filled. At first glance, it appeared to Ray that the occupant of that bed might be a Japanese soldier. The man was emaciated, with dark weathered skin and a vacant look in his eyes. His hair was short, perhaps recently shaved. Ray wondered why they would put a Japanese soldier in the same ward with him and his Allied brothers.

He looked at the man and felt a faint glimmer of recognition, but could not put his finger on the identity of the emaciated man in the other bed. Ray tentatively approached the bed and looked more closely at the stranger. As Ray looked at the man's face, the man looked up at him and said "Ray? Is that you?"

"Tom, is that you?" Ray replied.

Ray could hardly believe what had happened. Tom Tschirhart, looking much worse for the wear, had been rescued and was now placed into the bed directly across from his best friend, Ray Laenen! The two men cried for joy and marveled at the circumstances that had taken them from St. Rose High School and the east side of

Detroit, to a Liberty Ship on the Indian Ocean and now, to the same ward of a hospital in Perth, Australia.

Tom's lifeboat was the last boat to be rescued – thirty-two days after the sinking of the *Silvester*. An American submarine, the *USS Rock*, had picked up his boat on March 10, 1945. The rescue almost did not happen because the crew of the *USS Rock* thought that the boat merely contained local fishermen, and initially passed it by. They only returned to the little boat when they saw the men aboard waving frantically to them.

Tom Tschirhart and rescued crewmembers on
deck of the submarine USS Rock

Amazingly, although Tom's boat was the last to be rescued, they had actually made it closest to shore. They were only about twenty miles off the coast of Australia when the submarine sighted them. After the men were safely aboard the sub, it was necessary to sink the lifeboat. It could not be towed or lifted aboard the submarine. The boat that had kept Tom Tschirhart and his friends alive for thirty-two days was sent to Davey Jones' Locker by friendly fire from the 20mm and 40mm machine guns of the *USS Rock*.

Five of the seven Michigan men from Ft. Riley were now together again in Perth, Australia. Only Chuck Briley, the man who couldn't wait to get home to his sweetheart Marie, didn't make it. Ray Laenen, Don Tuthill, Chuck Kemmer and *The Three Toms* – Tschirhart, Spicketts and Morawski - had each survived an unthinkable horror and the uncertain hope of rescue from their small boats.

Tom Morawski and Ray in Perth, 1945

Young men of eighteen to twenty years typically have a surplus of resiliency in both body and spirit. As the Michigan men's wounds began to heal, they once again became playful and sociable. Their relief at being rescued gradually gave way to a restlessness to get out of the hospital.

Late one evening, Tom Spicketts had an idea. He and Ray wanted to get out and see the town, but didn't want to go through the bureaucratic paperwork necessary to secure a brief leave from the facility. Spicketts was, in many instances, the comedic agitator of the group, and was always looking for a new way to have some fun.

"Hey," said Tom, "why should we bother with all of that paperwork? After all, the wall is only six to eight feet tall (it was actually closer to twelve feet). We can climb over it easily, no problem."

Ray agreed, and the two sneaked out the hospital door and headed straight for the imposing wall. Neither knew what it might be like on the other side of the wall. Tom went over first.

"Is it OK for me to jump over?" asked Ray.

"Sure, come on over Amigo," answered his buddy, "everything is OK."

Ray hauled his freshly nourished body up and over the wall only to land, hands first, on a pile of broken bottles. The vault resulted in a severe gash on his hand – more severe than any of the wounds he had suffered when his ship was blown out of the water.

"Didn't you know about the broken bottles?" Ray asked.

"Sure," said Tom, "but I didn't think you'd land on them!"

Tom laughed heartily, but as these things go, Ray would not laugh about the incident until years later. He still has the scar on his hand, but now enjoys telling this vignette of the story of his friendship with Tom Spicketts.

The men spent about five months recovering in Perth. Aside from the date of April 12, 1945, when they received news that their Commander-in-Chief, Franklin D. Roosevelt, had died, it was a relatively uneventful period for the men of the 1st Regiment. It would be nice to say that after surviving such a harrowing ordeal, they were immediately returned safely to the United States. This, of course, did not happen. There was still a war going on, and Uncle Sam needed men to finish the job. The army used a points system to determine when a soldier would go home. Neither Ray nor *The Three Toms* had enough points to be discharged. In late July 1945, the men of the 1st regiment were told to pack up and hit the road – or in this case, the railroad tracks. They were going to travel by rail across the continent to Brisbane, and then to God only knows where.

Chapter Nine

Back into the Breach

It ain't over till it's over
– Yogi Berra

A ustralia's rail system in 1945 was not yet up to modern standards. In order to traverse the 2,500-mile continent, the men had to take two different kinds of trains. The first 1,200 miles or so were spent aboard an old narrow-gauge rail line. At about the halfway point of the journey, they transferred to a more modern standard-gauge railway train. Ultimately, they made it all the way across the continent to Brisbane. Although Brisbane is now known as "The Gold Coast" of Australia, it was not much to write home about at the time.

Brisbane, Australia 1945

After spending about two weeks in Brisbane, the men were ordered to board a troop ship bound for points unknown. Having survived the sinking of one large ship, some of the men were apprehensive about boarding another one. Ray didn't mind, he assumed that the risks went with the territory. The same optimism that made him certain of rescue several months earlier now gave him the confidence to board another ship without reservation.

The troop ship sailed north toward the island of New Guinea. Once they had cleared New Guinea, the men were informed of their destination. They were headed to the Philippines, which would be the launching point for the planned massive invasion of Japan. There would be no free passes for the men of the 1st Regiment. Thirty-two soldiers had died aboard the SS Peter Silvester, and the rest had survived with an assortment of physical and emotional scars. Now they would return to the front lines for what was expected to be the bloodiest battle of the entire war. Every available soldier was needed for this one, even those who had served at Normandy and Bastogne.

Along the way, in early August, the ship made a stop at the tiny island of Morotai, which is located in the Pacific Ocean about halfway between New Guinea and the Philippine Island of Mindanao. MacArthur had taken Morotai back from the Japanese the previous September, and it now served as a much-needed "leapfrog" airbase for the Allies. While on the island, some of the pilots took Ray and his friends up for rides on Mitchell B-25 bombers – the same type of planes used three years earlier for Colonel Jimmy Doolittle's bombing raids over Tokyo.

As the ship left Morotai, the men knew that their next stop would be in the Philippines, where they would engage the Japanese in perhaps the toughest battle yet. Soon after they left port, however, they received word that the Americans had dropped "some kind of really big bomb" on Japan. The significance of this event was not lost on Ray Laenen. He recalls with a sense of relief that can be felt even today, "The war ended while we were on that ship."

Though some may debate the ethics or necessity of dropping atomic bombs on the Japanese cities of Hiroshima and Nagasaki, no one can argue against the fact that these events directly hastened the end of the war, and avoided a bloody battle that neither side would have wanted. By the time Ray's troop ship landed in Manila, MacArthur had already accepted the surrender of the Japanese aboard the battleship *USS Missouri*.

Once ashore in Manila, the men were housed in a tent camp for a few days, until they received their assignments. Ray and Tom Tschirhart were both assigned to work as clerks at the bullet-riddled

Armed Forces Western Pacific (AFWESPAC) Headquarters. Once again, it seemed that no matter what happened, the two friends were destined to remain together. Tom Morawski was also assigned to work at AFWESPAC. At the time, Ray did not yet know how to type, but could hunt and peck with the best of them.

Bullet-riddled AFWESPAC Headquarters in Manila

Tom Spicketts was the only one of *The Three Toms* to be sent somewhere else. It was the only time from basic training to discharge that he was separated from the other Michigan men with whom he had shared this amazing experience.

Spicketts was sent instead, to work as an MP at Camp John Hay in the mountain village of Baguio. This was a most prized assignment as Baguio was high in the mountains, and therefore much cooler than the sweltering city of Manila. It also didn't hurt that the splendid accommodations were originally built to serve the few wealthy Filipinos who could afford such a sumptuous summer getaway. Even war weary troops were often sent to Baguio for rest and relaxation. Spicketts admits that this was a gravy assignment.

"Everybody wanted to go there," he said. "They had bowling alleys and golf courses. Since the war was over, I didn't really have much to do."

Chuck Kemmer was also sent to Manila. He recalls one incident regarding his friend Ray that stands out. "After we were rescued and sent to the Philippines, no one had any records, everything was lost with the ship. They needed to know where to assign all of us, so we all had to take an intelligence test. Well, Ray's test score was so high, that they thought he had cheated. They called him in and demanded to know where he got the answers to the test. Ray insisted that he was innocent so they made him retake the test. On the second try, he scored just as high as the first time. Compared to the rest of us, Ray was just really bright."

Shortly after his arrival in Manila, Ray decided to see some of the historic - if not infamous - locales in the Philippines where his military brothers had fought earlier battles. He and three friends set out one day in a jeep and went to visit two sites where American soldiers had suffered tremendous losses: Bataan and Corregidor. At the small island of Corregidor, Ray walked inside the tunneled fortress that had failed to protect the American soldiers against a massive Japanese onslaught in May of 1942. The Americans held out inside "The Rock" for as long as they could, and then surrendered to the Japanese. As Ray walked through the now eerily peaceful tunnels, he visualized the terror that his predecessors must have experienced while trapped inside their rock fortress.

Ray on a sightseeing trip to Bataan, 1945

At Bataan, Ray and his friends got out of the jeep and walked over part of the same road where, in April, 1942, twelve-thousand American (and 63,000 other) captured soldiers were marched by the Japanese a distance of sixty miles to an internment camp. The brutality of the Japanese soldiers during this walk was such that it will forever be remembered as the "Bataan Death March." Soldiers were routinely beaten and humiliated by their Japanese captors. Some who were starving and dehydrated were forced to continue marching past cool flowing water wells. In all, about ten-thousand men died before ever reaching their destination. Ray remembered seeing films of this atrocity on *Movietone News* reels when he was still a student at St. Rose. The images had served to steel the Americans' resolve to defeat the Japanese.

As Ray walked over that dirt road, he characteristically gave thanks once more to God for the blessings he had received – in contrast to the poor souls who had lost their lives at Bataan.

"I thought," he said, "there, but for the grace of God, go I. Every morning I thank God for the wonderful life he has given me. I think of this every morning when I am kneeling in church."

Ray didn't mind it so much at the AFWESPAC Headquarters. The building in which he worked was still heavily pockmarked by bullet holes from the February 1945 battle that took Manila back from the Japanese. While just about every soldier would rather be back home in a comfortable bed (considering the alternative), being a clerk in an Army office - with the war over - was not bad work if you could get it. Still, two of *The Three Toms* who were in the Philippines with Ray wound up going home early, each for different reasons.

Tom Morawski went home early when his mother died. Sadly, Ray learned about Mrs. Morawski's death before Tom did. One slow afternoon, the men were reading their mail from home. As previously mentioned, Ray's mother wrote him everyday. The mail typically arrived weeks, and sometimes months, after it was written. As he read his mother's account of the latest hometown news, Ray learned that Mrs. Laenen had gone to the funeral home the previous day to pay her respects to the recently deceased Mrs. Morawski. This surprised Ray because Tom had said nothing about his mother dying. Surely he would have told Ray if had he known that his own mother had died. Ray hoped that it would not be up to him to break the news to Tom. He hoped that Tom was reading the same thing right now in his own mail. Ray mustered up enough courage to ask "Hey Tom, how's the mail today?"

"Oh, same as usual" Tom replied matter-of-factly.

Tom's response clearly showed that he did not know of his mother's death. Letting the letter speak for itself, Ray handed his own letter to Tom and asked him to read it.

"Oh my God, my mother died!" said Tom.

A chaplain arranged for Tom to go home on an emergency leave. It was too late for him to attend his mother's funeral, but he was able to be with his family during their time of mourning. On that visit, Tom also met and fell in love with Agnes, the woman who would become his wife. He also got to stay home for good. Because the war was now over and Tom had already served almost two years, there was no need to send him back to the Philippines; Tom was honorably discharged without having to return to Manila.

Tom Tschirhart also went home early, but by an altogether different route. At that time, the Army still wanted soldiers to re-enlist. As an inducement, if you re-upped, you would be allowed to go home immediately for an extended furlough, and then you could choose where you would be deployed when you returned. Since the war was over, this sounded like a good deal to many men. Of course, the hitch was that you would be in the Army Reserves for a period of five years after you got out.

Tom was very homesick and wanted to take the deal. Even if he had to come back into the service, at least he would not have to wait a whole year to see his family. Ray, having learned his lesson from Tom's earlier scheme to switch high schools, thoughtfully declined the offer. He would serve his time, and then go home with no further service obligation.

Tom wanted to go home badly, so he decided to re-enlist, attached strings and all. A re-enlistment, however, would require a new physical before he could be enlisted into the "regular" army. Tom reported for that physical at the Santo Tomas Hospital in Manila. To his surprise, the examining doctor, after hearing about his ordeal aboard the *SS Peter Silvester*, and confirming his wounds, recommended a full medical discharge. Instead of re-joining the Army, Tom Tschirhart was discharged completely – with a full medical pension to boot! And one more thing: in order to aid in his recuperation, Tom was sent to the temporary Ashford General Hospital in West Virginia – better known today as the world-famous and luxurious Greenbrier Hotel. Later in his life, Tom would develop a case of peripheral neuritis, which in all likelihood originated from the immersion foot he suffered when he was adrift in the lifeboat.

Life in the Philippines was not necessarily bad for Ray Laenen. After working as a clerk at AFWESPAC for six months, he fell into a somewhat more interesting assignment.

A clerk's life is not a bad one, but there was even better work to be had. One of Ray's friends had the enviable job of being chauffeur to a brigadier general. Rather than slave all day over a hot typewriter, he got to drive around in a big Plymouth sedan and hobnob with the Army brass. One day, this friend told Ray that he had received his orders to go home, and the general wanted him to find a replacement chauffeur. He asked Ray if he would be interested in the job. Ray, of course, knew a good thing when he saw it, and immediately volunteered to replace his friend. He was introduced to Brigadier General Edward J. McGaw, a ruggedly handsome man from New Mexico who wore the characteristic thin moustache so popular with Hollywood actors of the time. General McGaw spent a few moments getting to know Ray Laenen and then hired him on as his chauffeur. He also gave him an immediate promotion to the rank of corporal. His new living quarters would be at the *Wac-Wac Country Club* in a nice part of Manila. After the ordeal Ray had recently endured in the Indian Ocean, things were beginning to look up.

General McGaw

Ray remembers General McGaw to be "a nice man, easy to get along with." His engaging personality and good looks also made him popular with the ladies. In addition to driving him on "official business," Ray also chauffeured him to the occasional *unofficial* meeting with a young lady who was either a government worker or a member of the Women's Air Corps (WAC). Ray would be instructed to drop the general off at a designated location and pick him up some two or three hours later. In the interim, the car was all Ray's. Ray reveled in the freedom that this gave him. He would drive the car to the Non-Commissioned Officers (NCO) club and hang out with his buddies until it was time to pick up the general again. One day, the general wanted to be driven up to Baguio. Ray used this opportunity to get together with his good friend Tom Spicketts. What a fantastic perk for a nineteen-year-old from Detroit who did not yet own his own set of wheels.

Ray strikes a pose with General McGaw's car

During his stay in Manila, as was common with many soldiers, Ray developed friendships with some of the local young Filipino women. The first was a young woman named Hope Jones who worked in the same office as Ray. She had been married to an American soldier who was killed during the war, and was now raising their young child alone. Her real name was Esperanza Jones, but everyone called her Hope, the English translation of her name. Ray and Hope were good friends who went to dinner occasionally, but nothing especially romantic came of the relationship.

A somewhat closer relationship developed between Ray and a young woman named Pacita Francisco, whom he had met at the Enlisted Men's Club. Given Ray's enviable work assignment, he frequently had use of General McGaw's car for their dates. They could travel anywhere they liked, in style. It was not, however, what you might think. All outings with Pacy were closely chaperoned by her protective mother, who rode happily in the back seat of McGaw's big Plymouth Sedan. Ray claims to this day that it didn't bother him a bit. After all, he liked Mrs. Francisco, and his intentions were strictly honorable. He felt like one of the family, and even mourned with them when Pacy's cousin died of skin cancer while Ray was still on his tour of duty in Manila.

Ray and Pacy after Mass in Manila

Lingoy, Mrs. Francisco and Pacy

This new position also gave Ray the opportunity to participate in one of the most historic moments in the history of The Philippines. The Philippine Islands had been under foreign control since the sixteenth century when they were vanquished by the Spanish Conquistadors. Control passed to the United States in 1898 as the result of the Spanish-American War. In 1941, the day after the Japanese bombed Pearl Harbor, they struck the Philippines. A month later the small nation was under the rule of the dangerously imperialistic Japan. This would remain so until the Philippines were liberated by the Americans in 1945. This time, however, the United States would finally return the Philippines to its own people. The date of July 4, 1946 for Philippine independence was not coincidental. The two countries, sharing an enduring bond of friendship, would now celebrate their respective dates of independence on the same day.

Philippine Independence Day was a long time in coming, and was celebrated greatly by both the Filipino people and the American military personnel who were helping to facilitate the transition. Ray's new position allowed him to be right in the thick of this historic event. He drove General McGaw's car in the Independence Day parade – just a few cars behind that of General Douglas MacArthur and his family. Ray still brims with excitement as he recalls the day.

"After the parade we went up into the reviewing stand, where I got to sit very near General MacArthur," he said. If the sinking of the SS Peter Silvester was the nadir of Ray Laenen's military experience, then this was surely the zenith. Perhaps the icing on the cake was the day General Eisenhower made a visit to AFWESPAC and Ray was able salute him from arm's length.

General Eisenhower salutes the troops at AFWESPAC Headquarters

While in the Philippines, Corporal Laenen had a bout with bronchial pneumonia which required a brief hospitalization, but other than that he remained healthy and in good spirits. He received two more promotions during his assignment in the Philippines, and would end his tour of duty as Staff Sergeant Remie Laenen. The young Belgian immigrant and athlete/scholar from St. Rose High School had come a long way indeed. In August 1946 – one year after arriving in Manila and two years after joining the service - Ray got word that he would be going home. He could hardly wait to see his family and start his new life.

Chapter Ten

Coming Home at Last

To an open house in the evening
Home shall men come
To an older place than Eden
And a taller town than Rome.
– G.K. Chesterton

The men returned home on the *SS Marine Panther* transport ship. You could chalk it up to youth and a wartime mentality that these young men who had almost lost their lives when their ship was sunk by German torpedoes, now would happily board yet another large ship. At least this time there would be no one shooting at them.

As Ray was gathering his belongings for the trip home, he stumbled upon an envelope that had fallen on the floor. It contained some snapshots. Ray asked around to determine if anyone nearby had dropped it, but there were no takers. He asked his commanding officer what to do with the packet, and the officer told him to keep it. Everyone was anxious to go home, and whoever lost the photos would not be delayed or left behind for a few personal photographs.

Ray examined the snapshots and was amazed at the images they contained. One was a snapshot print of what would become Joe Rosenthal's Pulitzer Prize winning photo of the flag-raising at Iwo Jima. Another showed General MacArthur accepting the Japanese surrender aboard the *USS Missouri*. Still others documented the ravages and atrocities of the battlefield.

There were snapshots of dead Japanese soldiers. Another gruesome photo showed an Asian man holding up the head of a Japanese soldier – impaled on a stake. These were historic pictures, painful images and sights that Ray was lucky to have never witnessed firsthand. In retrospect, Ray can only guess that the photos were the property of an army or press photographer (perhaps Joe Rosenthal himself) or a highly placed officer. Either way, it was time to go home.

As is often the case when one is most anxious to reach a destination, unexpected obstacles emerged to prolong the sendoff. The men aboard the *Marine Panther* were supposed to sail directly from Manila to the sunny coast of California. They got there, but not before a brief but frustrating diversion. It seems that one man aboard ship was thought to have contracted polio (this was in the pre-vaccination days) and so the entire ship was diverted to Yokohama, Japan where the men were held under a three-day quarantine to determine whether this was an isolated incident or an epidemic. As it turned out, the man did not have polio, and the ship was allowed to continue on its journey.

*Ray sits at the depot waiting to board the
SS Marine Panther for the ride home*

Tom Spicketts is ready to go home

The *Marine Panther* eventually set anchor in San Francisco Bay, and Ray Laenen was back in the United States at last. Ironically, a visitor from the Philippines waited at the dock to greet him on American soil. Pacita Francisco had a twin sister who had married an American man and was now living in San Francisco. As the ship pulled in to the dock, she waved to Ray from below as if to acknowledge the special bond that existed between their families – and their countries.

The SS Marine Panther arriving in San Francisco

At the age of twenty, Ray Laenen had already accumulated the kind of experiences that most men do not gather in a lifetime. He had served his adopted country in war, and brought home a Purple Heart Medal, a Victory Medal, an Asiatic Pacific Theater Ribbon with one Bronze Battle Star, three Overseas Service Bars and a Good Conduct Medal. The experience had strengthened, not diminished, his love for this country. That devotion to the *Land of the Free* would grow with every subsequent year until it would later crystallize into an unabashed and unapologetic patriotism.

From San Francisco, a train shipped the men to Fort Lewis, Washington, where Staff Sergeant Remie Laenen was honorably discharged from the United States Army on August 21, 1946. He and Tom Spicketts (the only one of *The Three Toms* who had not been discharged early) headed for home on another train. At a brief stop in Colorado, the men were told that they had a little time to kill and could disembark for a while. Denver is hot in the summer, and Spicketts got a sudden urge for some ice cream. Problem was, he had lost all of his money playing poker with some other soldiers. Years later, looking back at his situation, he offered this sage advice: "You don't want to gamble with people you don't know."

Tom Spicketts and Ray celebrate their discharge from the U.S. Army

"Ray," he said, "they're selling ice cream up there. Give me some money and I'll go get us some." A nice cold pint of ice cream sounded just right to Ray at the time, so he gave Amigo the cash. Several minutes later, Spicketts returned to the train, but without the ice cream. He was licking the last remnants off of the carton when Ray asked him where his ice cream went.

"It was starting to melt," Tom rationalized, so I had to eat it all myself." Ray was out the money and the ice cream, but somehow things like that don't matter too much when you are on your way home.

They completed the trip across the American plains and finally to the Michigan Central Depot Station in Detroit, where Ray's parents waited to take him home. At last.

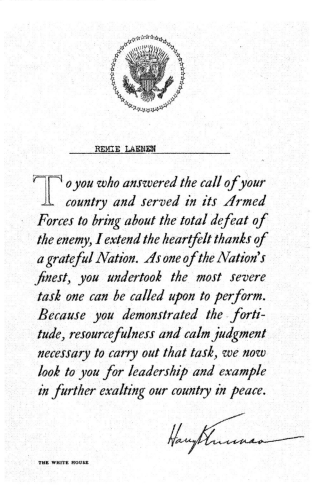

Thank you letter from President Harry S. Truman

It may surprise some to learn that there was no welcome home party thrown at the house on Hillger Street when Ray Laenen walked through the door. This was, after all, as Tom Brokaw has so aptly described, *The Greatest Generation*. Everything including war was taken, for the most part, in stride. Perhaps in part weary from the war, and perhaps just inhabitants of another time when sacrifice and honor were the rule, not the exception, the Laenens welcomed their son home but did not overdo the celebration. And still, something happened that night that would change Ray's life forever.

During Ray's absence, Gustaf and Josephine had maintained their friendships with the Tschirharts and other members of Detroit's Belgian community. One family that they had become close to was the DeMeulemeesters. As it was, on the evening Ray returned home, Norma DeMeulemeester had been out on a date, but returned to the Laenen's home where her parents were visiting. Ray had not seen her since before he went into the service, but when he did, it was an epiphany. That little girl who had thrown snowballs at him behind her uncle's bar, and then later entered his social sphere as just one of the gang, was now a vision to behold. Ray describes that initial reunion with just three words: "I was smitten."

Luckily for Ray, the feeling was mutual and the two began dating again, this time much more seriously. Things never looked better for the American war veteran from Oevel, Belgium. The war was behind him, he was in love, and it was time for him to find his piece of the American Dream.

Chapter Eleven

Finding the American Dream

If one advances confidently in the direction of his dreams, and endeavors to live the life which he has imagined, he will meet with success unexpected in common hours.
– Henry David Thoreau

As time went by, Ray and Norma knew that they would eventually marry. In the nineteen forties, however, first things came first. Most men at that time would not think of getting married without having a steady job and a means to support a family. Ray's first step would be to get a college education, and the GI Bill afforded him the means to do so. As it was, Tom Tschirhart and some of the other St. Rose gang had been making plans to attend the now defunct Detroit Business University, (not to be confused with the locally extant Detroit Business Institute) which was located downtown in the Book Tower. DBU sounded just fine to Ray, so he enrolled in the university's commercial science program, where he studied accounting, marketing and business. Ever the achiever, he completed a Bachelor of commercial science degree in just over three years.

Meanwhile, Ray's love for Norma was in full bloom. About six months after they began dating, Norma and her mother went back to Oeselgem, Belgium, to visit Mrs. DeMeulemeester's elderly mother. Oeselgem is located about halfway between Antwerp, Belgium, and Aachen, Germany. Taking a cue from his own mother, Ray wrote a letter to Norma every day that she was gone – a total of three months.

Shortly after Norma returned from Belgium, Ray's father was summoned to Belgium by his siblings, who informed him that his mother was gravely ill and would not likely make it through the coming winter. Gustaf and Josephine flew to Belgium in July of 1947. Ray had, by that time, begun attending college and could not go with his parents on this trip. He did not know that it would be the last time he would see his father alive.

Gustaf was very proud of the brand new stainless steel wheelchair he had bought to bring to his mother. She had been using an old wooden one and the new one would be much easier to ambulate. One morning, six weeks after arriving in Oevel, Gustaf felt ill after eating his breakfast. Assuming that it was just indigestion, he told his family that he was going out to the backyard to drink some spa water and have some fresh air. Ray received a phone call from his mother later that day informing him that his father had died of a heart attack. At the age of fifty-two, Gustaf Laenen had died in the place where he was born, and was buried in Belgium. His strand, however, was already firmly entwined in the American rope, and his progeny would continue without him in America. Gustaf's mother, as had been predicted, died later that winter.

Perhaps the last photo ever taken of Gustaf Laenen
as he waits with Josephine to board an airplane to Antwerp.
He was bringing the wheelchair to his ailing mother.

Remie Laenen married his snowball-throwing sweetheart Norma DeMeulemeester at St. Paul's Catholic Church in Grosse Pointe, Michigan on February 19, 1949. Joe Laenen served as best man, and two of *The Three Toms* stood up for their good friend. Tom Morawski couldn't make it, as his wife was five-months pregnant at the time.

Wedding photo of Ray and Norma Laenen

The newlyweds planned a honeymoon in the ski resort town of Uniontown, Pennsylvania. At the time, Ray owned an old Chevrolet that, with God's help, might or might not have made it all the way to Pennsylvania. Luckily, the newlyweds would not have to worry about that. Norma's mother and brother had "bought" them a brand new, midnight blue 1949 Ford convertible as a wedding gift. The catch was that Ray and Norma would have to take over the payments on the vehicle - minus the generous down payment that had already been made. The new couple was thrilled, and hit the road, fully stocked with luggage, skis and the American Dream now within their sight.

The 1949 Ford parked outside a honeymoon motel

Uniontown was a well-known ski area, but when the Laenens arrived at the Summit Hotel, they could see no snow. They wondered where all of the snow was hiding. Perhaps, they thought, it was higher up in the mountains. No, they soon found out, there was no snow. The hotel manager apologized profusely (for something over which he had absolutely no control) and tried to comfort the weary travelers with photos of the resort in much snowier times.

"This is how it is supposed to look," he assured them as he showed off the wintry photos.

Taking the lack of snow as a sign, the Laenens made one of their first major decisions as a married couple – they took their winter ski equipment and drove all the way down to sunny Florida. One can only wonder what the residents of that snowless state thought of the sight of the two vacationers arriving in a car packed with ski equipment.

Soaking up the sun in Florida – but where are the snow skis?

Good fortune continued to smile on the Laenens when they returned to Michigan. One of the biggest decisions a new couple must make is where to live. For most at that stage of life, an apartment or flat is the best that one can hope for. Ray and Norma, of course, were luckier than most.

The newlyweds take a chauffeur driven ride around
Washington D.C. while on their way to Florida

Norma's parents had divorced about a year before she and Ray were married. In happier times, the family had bought a beautiful old lakefront home just north of Detroit on Jefferson Avenue in St. Clair Shores. The home is a local landmark, which was built in the 1920s with a castle-like appearance and beautiful stonework. Both the stones and the masons who set the stones were imported from the Cotswold area of England specifically for the construction of this home. Now, with Mr. DeMeulemeester gone, there was no way that Norma's mother could possibly care for the large house by herself. She suggested that Ray and Norma live with her in the house. They accepted, and to this day have never lived anywhere else.

The arrangement was not as difficult as one might suspect. Ray got along very well with his mother-in-law, and besides, she was often gone from the home when Ray was there. At the time, she had been helping Norma's brother run his bar. "Dee's Bar" was located at Mack Avenue and Lycaste, just a few blocks from St. Rose

High School. Mrs. DeMeulemeester managed the afternoon shift and came home after 2:00 AM, while Ray worked elsewhere on days. Ray and Norma rarely saw Mrs. DeMeulemeester, except on weekends. All in all, if was a great arrangement for everyone.

In 1949, Ray got his first *real* job, as a salesman for Clary Multiplier, a company that sold adding machines and cash registers. As with many first jobs, it was a good opportunity that didn't pay especially well. About a year later, Ray's brother Joe approached him with an idea. The owner of Vinci's Market in the old neighborhood at the corner of Hillger and Goethe was planning to retire and sell the store. Ray knew the store well, as he had shopped there often and worked there briefly as a stockboy when he was 16 years old. Ray liked his job at Clary Multiplier, but knew that it would be difficult to support a family on his current earnings. At the time, the Laenens had just had their first child, Gary. Ray decided to leave the security of his current job for the gamble of making more money as the co-owner of a neighborhood grocery store.

Ray (left) and Joe inside Laenen's Market

Joe and Ray bought the store in 1950 and renamed it *Laenen's Market*. During that time, the Laenen family grew quickly - as any good Catholic family would. Gary had been born in March of 1950. Their second child, Rick, was born a year later. Then came Bob, and then Carrie, and finally, Kim. Ray and Norma Laenen, good Catholics that they were, were to have five children within the first six years of their marriage. By the time Rick was born, Ray realized that the small grocery store would never produce enough income to support both his family and Joe's family. He needed something that would pay better.

Ray stands in front of Laenen's Market

As so often happened in Ray's life, the right circumstances always seemed to arise just when he needed them. Norma's cousin, Lee (her previously mentioned snowball partner), worked for Motor Products Inc., an automotive parts supplier in Detroit. One day in

1952, Lee called Ray to tell him that an assistant auditor position had opened up at the company. Ray's degree and background made him a perfect candidate for the position. He interviewed, and got the job. In July 1952, after two years as a grocery store owner, Ray became an assistant auditor for Motor Products, Inc. and left *Laenen's Market* to his brother Joe. It was a win-win situation for both. Joe could do better without having to split the profit two ways, and Ray could support his growing family with the new, better paying job. As it turned out, Joe gave up the store a year later and went to work as a salesman - for Clary Multipliers!

Ray stayed at Motor Products for about two years, during which time he was promoted into the purchasing department. His job was to act as a liaison to the eleven different companies that supplied steel to Motor Products. Ray traveled the country and forged good relations with his client companies. That small promotion would give him the skills and, later, the opportunities that would, in time, enable him to fulfill the American Dream.

In 1955, after about three years in this job, the company was sold and the employees given six months notice to find other work. Just as Ray began to question the wisdom of his move, opportunity presented itself once again.

George Burley, the director of purchasing at Motor Products told Ray of a good job that had opened up at Cummins Diesel in Columbus, Indiana. It was another purchasing position, but at a much larger company with a much larger salary. Ray interviewed for the position first in Detroit and then at the corporate headquarters in Indiana. The company requested that Norma also be present at that second interview. She agreed, and was interviewed and introduced to several of the other wives of the executives. At that time, a man's wife was sometimes thought to be an integral part of his resume.

Norma was, fortunately, much more than that. As she recalled later, "I passed the test, but I didn't like it. It was too pretentious for me."

As the old saying goes, *watch what you ask for, because you may get it.* At the completion of the interview process, Ray was offered a position that would include a salary about double what he was then making, membership in an exclusive country club and all the trappings of a corporate executive position.

This new opportunity posed a serious dilemma for the Laenen family. Accepting the position would mean selling the house and moving to Indiana – away from the support of the close families and community to which they were well connected. And yet, how could he turn down such a lucrative offer, especially when his family was growing and he was sure to lose his current job within a few months?

Norma, always the independent spirit, politely expressed some reservations about all of the downsides to accepting this position, not the least of which was her reluctance to accept the role of being a 1950s corporate wife. She was not quite sure that she would be comfortable with the corporate politics and country club atmosphere of the new position.

"I've never been someone who likes cocktail parties and all that baloney," she said candidly.

Also, what would they do with Mrs. DeMeulemeester who was still living with them in the St. Clair Shores home? With his wife's (and his own) misgivings hanging like a storm cloud over his head, he reluctantly made the decision to accept the new position anyway. He went down to Indiana one week to begin looking for a house and a Catholic school for his children. His search proved productive and he ended the week with a down payment on a new house and his two oldest children enrolled in a local Catholic School.

Just when he returned to St. Clair Shores, providence stepped boldly (once more) into his life, this time in the form of a newspaper article. As he perused the Sunday *Detroit Free Press*, one headline leapt off of the page like a hot spark. *"So You Want to be The Spouse of a Corporate Executive?"* it challenged the reader. With his interest solidly piqued, Ray read the article. It confirmed all of Norma's fears about what she might expect as a corporate executive's wife. Ray interpreted the article as another clear case of divine intervention. "It was as if God was saying 'Hey Mr. Laenen, you'd better think this over carefully."

Ray and Norma took this sign for what it was and made the decision to stay where they were. Ray apologized to the people at Cummins Diesel, and told them that he had changed his mind and would not be coming to Indiana after all.

Luckily, there were other job opportunities in the healthy post-war economy of Detroit. Ray landed a job with Trevor Steel, a supplier to Motor Products Inc. The new owner of Trevor Steel was the son of the chairman of the board of Motor Products. Ray now identifies this job as the start of his long career in the steel industry. The plan was to start Ray in the warehouse, and then in about a year move him into sales. He actually moved into sales within three months.

Ray did well in sales, and landed many large accounts including the contract for the General Motors Truck and Bus Division. One day, a man named Kurt Hartlieb, who was the director of purchasing for Garland Manufacturing, another of Ray's clients, approached him. Like Ray, Kurt Hartlieb was not born in the United States. He had been born in Willemshaven, Germany in 1914, and moved to America in 1928. Hartlieb was a very bright and witty man who was articulate in both English and German. The two men shared a mutual respect for each other's background, character and abilities. Ray, being a man of practical and forgiving sensibilities, held no grudge against this man of German birth. Less than ten years had passed since Ray's ship had been sunk by German sailors, but to Ray, Kurt Hartlieb was every bit as American as he.

It seemed that Garland Manufacturing was about to pack up and close its Detroit facilities after its employees had decided to unionize. The new headquarters would be located about 150 miles north of Detroit in the rural community of West Branch, Michigan. Hartlieb did not want to relocate to West Branch, and asked Ray if he would be interested in forming a partnership to start their own steel company. It would be called Hartlieb-Laenen Steel Inc., with Kurt Hartlieb's name going first due to his age (he was twelve years older than Ray), experience, and greater financial commitment to start the company. At that time, Ray was not willing to take such a chance. He now had five children and was making a comfortable living at Trevor Steel. Large gambles were not a part of Ray Laenen's character. Such are the choices we make in life. Kurt Hartlieb opened his new company under the singular name Hartlieb Steel Inc.

Ray stayed at Trevor Steel for another year and a half while Kurt Hartlieb got his new company off the ground. In 1962, change was afoot once again at Trevor Steel. George Lott, the owner, had decided that in order to remain competitive in the future, Trevor Steel needed to go in a different direction. In order to capture a more exclusive market, they would begin specializing in niche steels like galvanized and stainless. Ray knew that for him, this would mean starting over from scratch. He would have to learn a whole new side of the business, and develop an entirely new clientele. Ray went back to see his friend Kurt Hartlieb.

Hartlieb was happy to see Ray again and still very interested in a partnership. He knew that Ray was a dynamic sales expert who could do wonders for the fledgling company. Now however, since Kurt had already invested countless time and effort in the new endeavor, they could not split the partnership quite as evenly as they had previously envisioned. The two men negotiated a satisfactory arrangement out of which a thirty-year partnership was born. As it turns out, Hartlieb was correct in his assessment of Ray Laenen's skills.

The initial agreement called for Ray to work strictly on commission for about a year, in order to raise the capital needed to buy into the partnership. After only six months on the job, Kurt Hartlieb conceded that Ray was making more money on commissions than he was making as the owner of the company. Ray bought into Hartlieb Steel and remained in partnership with Kurt Hartlieb until they sold the company in 1990. It was a deep friendship as much as a solid partnership that worked well for both men (and their families) on a financial and personal level.

Ray Laenen was never the type to take his blessings for granted. He retired from Hartlieb Steel when it was sold in 1990, but not a day went by that he did not literally and figuratively thank God for the blessings he has received in his lifetime. He used the occasion of his retirement to begin attending mass not just on Sundays, but now every day. Not one to spend his retirement days parked in front of a television set, Ray increased his involvement in the activities of St. Gertrude Parish. He and Norma have been parish members for over fifty years. During that time, Ray has served on the Ushers Club (as President), the Men's Club, and the Parish Council. He has served as a lector, and for nine years was the chairman of the Archdiocesan Development Fund. To this day, he can be seen praying and attending mass each morning at St. Gertrude Catholic Church.

Ray credits his success in family and business to everyone but himself. To God, for sparing his life on that treacherous night of February 6, 1945, in the Indian Ocean, and for giving him enough faith to last a lifetime. To his father, Gustaf, for having the foresight to see a great future in the land of the free, the United States of America. To his mother, Josephine, who instilled in him a desire for learning and a confidence in himself. To Norma, his wife and constant support through all of the good times and bad.

As his family grew, Ray Laenen relished his role as a husband and father. As is often the case, the family size outpaced the family income. The Laenens, however were both frugal and industrious. After making numerous trips to the barbershop for the four boys, Ray decided that he could save a considerable amount of money by cutting their hair himself. Norma bought a hair cutting set at J.L. Hudson's, and Ray tried his hand at the tonsorial arts. After one rather unsuccessful attempt on oldest son Gary, he conceded that "It became very apparent that Ray Laenen was not a potential barber!"

Norma took over and proved to be a more competent hand with a pair of scissors and an electric clipper – especially in the late fifties world of buzzcuts.

Each time Norma gave the boys a haircut, the Laenens would put away the sum of money that would have been spent on professional haircuts. The money was kept in a jar that they called the "Disneyland Piggy Bank." The plan was to save up enough for a family trip to the new amusement park that Walt Disney had opened in California in 1955. The Disneyland Piggy Bank received its first dollar in 1956, and by 1962 had swollen to an impressive eleven hundred dollars. The local banks had helped a little as Ray periodically took the contents of the jar to the bank, where it could earn additional interest. As promised, in 1962 the Laenen family at last made the long trip by car from Detroit to Anaheim, California, (by way of the old Route 66) where they enjoyed perhaps the most American of all types of entertainment, the theme park.

This dream vacation started a trend that pleased the family for years. Norma continued to cut the boys' hair, and Ray fed the "Disneyland Piggy Bank," which kept its name regardless of the destination for each subsequent year's vacation. In various years, the Laenen family took classic American road trips to places as near as Mackinac Island, Michigan, and as far away as Quebec City, Yellowstone National Park and the New York World's Fair. A trip to Weekie-Watchie in Florida proved so popular with the kids that the family repeated the vacation three years in a row. They hung a plasterboard map of the United States on a basement wall and updated it on a regular basis by placing pins in each spot they had visited. Nothing binds a large family together like a two-week road trip in one non-air-conditioned station wagon.

In 1966, the family took the one vacation that became the standard by which all future Laenen vacations would be measured. They went to Europe.

How they got from Detroit to Europe is worth noting. The airplane trip from New York across the Atlantic was routine, but the car ride from Detroit to New York was somewhat unusual. It seems that just prior to leaving for the trip, Ray had purchased a brand new 1966 Pontiac Bonneville convertible. With such a behemoth beauty sitting in the garage, the kids would have no part of another vacation in a common Ford Country Squire station wagon. They insisted that the family of seven cram themselves into the new convertible and ride to New York in style. It didn't take much to twist Ray's arm. The family made the long trip for the most part with the top down and the wind in their hair.

Before heading to Europe, they stopped off to visit with Stan Kleckner, another old army buddy that Ray had met while both were stationed in the Philippines.

The trip to Europe had a dual purpose. The first was to introduce the Laenen children to their Belgian relatives and the second was to make a pilgrimage to Lourdes, France. In one fell swoop, the children would learn something of their ethnic and religious heritage.

In Belgium, they stayed with a different relative almost every night. The Laenen and DeMeulemeester families would have no part of them staying in hotels. The kids got to meet all of the cousins, aunts and uncles who had remained in Belgium when the Laenens and Demeulemeesters had emigrated so many years before. The sidetrip to France was actually more than just a quick sightseeing tour. They traveled by bus, and stayed in France for a week. They visited Paris and Lyon before making the pilgrimage to the religious site of Lourdes, where the Virgin Mary is believed to have visited young Bernadette Soubirous in 1858. So what do the Laenen children remember most about this historic vacation? The fact that they ate chicken every single night of the trip. Such are the memories that endure.

Ray lost his mother Josephine in 1977. In another eerie coincidence, like her late husband Gustaf, Josephine died while she was out of town visiting a relative. She had gone down to Columbus, Ohio, to visit her son Joe, and to see the new house he had recently built. She got up in the middle of one night to use the bathroom and was found by the family the next morning. This time, Joe Laenen made the sad telephone call to inform his brother that their mother was dead. Ray felt the loss deeply, but also knew that he had a family whose love and support would see him through.

Many men and women look at life from the perspective of their failures, losses and the things they were not able to obtain or achieve. Not Ray Laenen, not even for a minute. Ray remains ever thankful for all that he has. In fact, he seems to be nourished by a deep, bottomless well of gratitude, one that he is happy to share with anyone who will listen. And share he does. As with most everything else in his life, he used the opportunity of his retirement as a means to give something back. Back to his family, his community and most of all to the country that he loves with an unabashed passion.

"I am so proud to be an American," he says. "I thank God that my parents had the courage to leave their families and their country to come here."

Chapter Twelve

A Time to Reflect,
A Time to Forgive

That best portion of a good man's life,
His little, nameless, unremembered acts
Of kindness and love
– William Wordsworth

The years rolled by, and like many other WWII combat veterans, Ray Laenen pushed the memories of his war experience into the back recesses of his mind. These memories never fade completely away of course, but without care and feeding, they eventually seem to take on a lesser importance. Eventually however, Ray, like so many others of his age group, began to take stock of those defining moments of his life. His service to America more than forty years earlier finally began to take on the importance it deserved. Now fully recognizing the historical gravity of their experiences and their contributions to our nation, the survivors of the *SS Peter Silvester* decided to get together for a reunion.

The first reunion was held in the summer of 1981 at the home of a man named Clinton House in Cleveland, Ohio. Many of the men had informally kept in contact over the years, and maintained friendships with each other. Ray had continued to keep in touch with *The Three Toms* and a few others from the ship. He had also maintained correspondence with Bob Taylor, one of the men from the *HMS Activity* who had helped in the rescue. This was the first time, however, since the sinking of the *Silvester* thirty-six years earlier, that the men had come together as a group. This meeting served to reactivate many of the memories that had lain dormant for so many years.

As the men traded stories and personal recollections, each would remember bits and pieces of details they hadn't thought about for a long time. Associations clicked and brought old memories back to the forefront. Gradually, ancient memories of a time past were conveyed (through the sharing of personal stories) into the present. Fresh new perspectives now helped to define the meaning of their lives. Being of that particular generation, these men had never allowed themselves to celebrate the importance of what they had done. Now they finally could - and did.

The reunion in Ohio

The following year, Ray Laenen organized a second reunion, this time at his home in St. Clair Shores, Michigan. On July 17, 1982, eleven survivors of the sinking of the *SS Peter Silvester* (including *The Three Toms*) gathered on the shores of beautiful Lake St. Clair to, once more, eat, drink and renew the bonds that once held them together in a life and death struggle against tyranny. Again, the men traded stories and jostled long lost pieces of memory back into their collective awareness.

After these men had raised families, built careers and otherwise took care of the business of life, they were finally able to step back and allow themselves the luxury of retrospection. Within that context, many of the men, for the first time, began to fully understand the significance of their accomplishments. They had each been an integral part of perhaps the most historical event of the twentieth century, World War II.

The reunion in Ray Laenen's back yard. Back row, L to R: Don Tuthill, Ray Laenen, Chuck Kemmer, Lt. Birch, Tom Morawski. Front row, L to R: Tom Tschirhart, Tom Spicketts, Cliff Hinton.

The wives at the reunion

For Ray Laenen, the reunions awakened a strong sense of patriotism and a desire to share his story with others. In remembering his own experiences and hearing the stories of other survivors of the *SS Peter Silvester*, Ray began to fully comprehend what he had always known – that freedom is not free.

A couple of years earlier, in 1979, Ray had spoken at the local Rotary chapter in neighboring Grosse Pointe about his WWII experiences. The talk went over well, and he soon began to expand his speaking engagements. On Veteran's Day, 1991, Ray was asked to speak to a class of eighth graders in Hadley, Michigan, near Lapeer. The invitation had come through the efforts of daughter Carrie, whose own daughter Melissa was in the class. Carrie was proud of her father's service to his country and knew that the children in Melissa's class would hear a story like they had never heard before.

The children listened in rapt astonishment as Ray told the story of the sinking of the *Peter Silvester*, and his twenty-two days adrift in the Indian Ocean. Animated and filled with emotion, Ray brought the story to life in a way that no textbook could ever match. After the presentation, he asked the children to remember the thirty-two men who lost their lives aboard the SS Peter Silvester, and then led the assembly in a spirited singing of the National Anthem.

*Ray pledges allegiance to the flag with schoolchildren
at Hadley Elementary School*

Later, the teachers and students of the school expressed their gratitude through hand-made thank-you notes and crayon drawings, which were presented to him a short time later. Most of the children's pictures showed representations of Ray, his lifeboat, or the *SS Peter Silvester* being torpedoed (naturally, a favorite of the boys). The outpouring of gratitude touched Ray deeply. He realized that most of the children had never heard a personal account of such drama, nor of the kind of sacrifice made by so many to ensure our freedom. He put all of the drawings and cards into a scrapbook, which he keeps now as one of his most treasured possessions.

Word eventually got around about Ray's ability to connect with the schoolchildren. He began to give other presentations to children around Memorial Day, Veteran's Day, or any other time that he was invited. At last count, he had spoken to various children's groups at least twenty-four times. The scrapbook of patriotic drawings continues to grow and is likely to continue for quite some time. It is clear that Ray gets at least as much out of these talks as the children get from hearing him.

At one time, Ray also made frequent trips back to old St. Rose School to talk to the nuns who had taught him so many years before. By this time, the actual school had closed and the building was now used as the St. Rose Senior Center. The center's administrator was Site Director Sr. Rose Bernadette, another IHM nun. Each time Ray made a visit, he walked up the stairway and stopped to pray at the bronze plaque that hung on the wall commemorating the eight St. Rose students who had been killed in WWII. The names of each soldier were listed on the plaque under the following inscription:

> *"For God and country, even unto death, these boys made the supreme sacrifice in World War II. May their souls rest in peace."*

Many times, tears would stream down Ray's cheeks as he prayed and remembered his fallen comrades.

"I thanked God," he said, "that my name and Tom Tschirhart's name were not on that plaque."

Ironically, one of the names on the St. Rose plaque was that of Neal Diehl. Neal had joined the army on the same day as Ray and Tom Tschirhart. In fact, Ray, Tom and Neal had walked together through the door of the recruiting office that day. Arriving together, Neal's service number was only one digit higher than Ray's. That one digit became the difference of life or death for the two men. While Ray and Tom were shipped out to Fort Riley, Kansas, on to the *SS Peter Silvester*, and then (eventually) safely home, Neal Diehl never came home. He was sent instead to the Philippines where he was killed in action fighting the Japanese.

The aptly named Sister Rose was very familiar with Ray and his attachment to the plaque. In 1996, when the school was to be sold to a private buyer, she and Ray feared that the plaque might not hold the same sentimental value with the new owners. Rather than let the plaque fall victim to the wrecking ball or get lost forever in someone's attic, they wanted to make sure that it would be preserved for posterity. Ray agreed to care for the plaque and kept it safely at his home until the summer of 2004, when he donated it to the archives of the Archdiocese of Detroit. He figured that the Archdiocese would be around a lot longer than he would, and the plaque would be in good hands for many years to come.

In 1995, Ray received something in the mail that would later lead to the most incredible of circumstances. Russ Hoover, another survivor of the *Silvester* sinking had sent Ray a copy of a Canberra, Australia, newspaper article by an Australian naval historian named David Stevens. Hoover had received the article from George "Rud" Rimes, an Australian Navy airman who had, in February 1945, participated in the air search and rescue operation to find the survivors of the *SS Peter Silvester.* Hoover was one of the raft survivors who had maintained contact with Rimes over the years. In the article, Stevens wrote about German U-boat activity off the coast of Australia during the latter part of the war. In particular, he wrote about the exploits of the *U-862*, its mission and its crew. Also, the article indicated that Stevens was in the process of writing a book about the *U-862*.

Ray was astonished that an Australian newspaper would publish a story about an event that was so central to his own life. He was also amazed that, in researching for his article, the author had spoken to some of the German men who had served aboard *the U-862*.

Ray immediately wrote a letter to Rimes and asked him if he could somehow get in touch with David Stevens. In part, he wanted to learn more details about the U-boat, and at the same time felt that he could provide some valuable first-person details regarding his own experience. Rimes supplied the address for David Stevens and Ray sent him a letter, including a copy of the 1980 article from the *Detroit Free Press.*

Stevens responded to Ray's letter in May 1995, touching off a chain of events that would reverberate from St. Clair Shores, Michigan, to Gummersbach, Germany. In his letter, Stevens thanked Ray for contacting him and asked if Ray would provide more information regarding his experience. In addition, Stevens offered to forward a letter to some of the remaining German crewmen of the *U-862*, if Ray was interested. He most certainly was.

In August 1995, David Stevens forwarded a letter Ray Laenen had written to Herr Albert Schirrmann who was a machinist aboard the *U-862*, and now resided somewhere in Germany. In the interest of privacy, Stevens kept Schirrmann's address to himself, so at the time, Ray had no idea where the German man lived.

In the letter, Ray introduced himself as a survivor of the sinking of the *SS Peter Silvester* and suggested that the two men might benefit from mutual correspondence to learn more about each other. Ray also made it clear that he held "no animosity" toward his former enemy, and in fact was grateful that the Germans did not kill the remaining survivors of his ship that night. The letter indicated that Ray understood that the two men were fighting for their respective countries, and each did what they had to do during a time of war. He included information about himself, and another copy of the *Detroit Free Press* article from 1980. After he mailed the letter, Ray felt hopeful, but knew that he would understand completely if Mr. Schirrmann did not wish to reply.

REMIE LAENEN

ST. CLAIR SHORES, MICHIGAN 48081

August 5, 1995

Mr. Albert Schirrmann

Dear Mr. Schirrmann:

First of all, I should begin my letter by introducing myself. My name is Remie (Ray) Laenen. I was one of the survivors of the sinking of the S.S. Peter Sylvestre which was torpedoed by the U-862 on February 6, 1945 in the Indian Ocean.

I have been informed by Mr. David Stevens of Canberra, Australia that you were a member of the U-862 crew as Maschineobergefreiten. Needless to say, I am fascinated by the fact that after fifty years has passed, I find my self corresponding with a crewman who was involved in the most memorable event in my life and which almost cost me my life.

Let me say at the outset, that I hold no animosity or grudge toward you. After all, at the time, our countries were at war and our duty and allegiance was to our respective country. In fact, I have always maintained a grateful and appreciative feeling toward your commander, Captain Timm, for not killing any of the survivors on that fateful night. As I sit here and reminisce, I can still see your submarine as it surfaced so closely to our lifeboat wondering if this would be the last day of my young life.

It is my desire to initiate an exchange of letter writing with you so that I may know a little about you. Ironically, my birthplace was a little village near Antwerp, Belgium. I immigrated to the U.S.A. at an early age with my parents and was inducted into the U.S. Army in July, 1944. I have traveled extensively, including three trips to Germany. One, as late as last year.

I have lived in the Detroit, Michigan area most of my life. I have been married 46 years, have 5 children and 11 grand-children. I have retired over 4 years. My profession was a businessman and partner in a steel brokerage company. In fact, my partner, Kurt Hartlieb, was German-born from the Wilhelmshaven area near the North Sea and who immigrated to the U.S.A. in 1928.

I would appreciate any information you might submit about yourself. Who knows, I may have been in your home area on one of my trips. As I mentioned, we have traveled throughout Germany rather extensively.

With that, I will conclude my letter in hopes that you will respond. In the meantime, "Auf Wiedersehn."

Best regards,

Ray Laenen

P.S. I am enclosing an article which appeared in a recent edition of our local paper, The Detroit Free Press. I think you will find It rather interesting. Also, if you prefer to correspond in German, I could easily have it translated by my partner who is very fluent in German.

Ray's letter to Albert Schirrmann

After a few weeks went by, a reply from the German sailor to Ray's letter seemed more and more unlikely. A month passed, then two, then three, still nothing. Ray accepted the fact that he would apparently never get a response to his letter.

One day in February of 1996, about six months after he had sent the original letter, Ray went out to check his mail. There was an envelope in the mailbox with the distinctive markings of overseas airmail. Still, this was nothing unusual. Ray had many relatives in Belgium, so it was nothing out of the ordinary to receive such envelopes in the mail. The return address indicated that the letter came from Denmark. Ray didn't know anyone in Denmark.

He opened the letter and found that it came from a woman named Monika Barse who lived with her husband and children in the town of Gentofte, near Copenhagen, Denmark. She identified herself as the stepdaughter of Albert Schirrmann, and said that she was replying on his behalf because he did not speak or write English very well. She wrote that her stepfather was very pleased to receive the letter from Ray, and had shown it to his family and friends at Christmas time. He had not replied sooner because he had recently undergone heart bypass surgery, and his health was deteriorating.

The letter indicated that Albert Schirrmann and the other seventeen remaining members of the *U-862* crew had remained in contact with each other and met once each year for a reunion – just as the crew of the *SS Peter Silvester* had done twice before. Mr. Schirrmann was kind enough to send Ray some photos of the ship and crew, with a copy of a page from his personal wartime diary - dated February 6, 1945. With this, a most unlikely friendship developed between the two former enemies – but by correspondence only, and on two different continents. The two men continued to correspond for the next year-and-a-half, but never had the chance to meet in person. In 1997, Albert Schirrmann died of a heart attack while shopping at a supermarket in Germany.

Albert Schirrmann and his wife

Once again, Monika Barse served as intermediary to inform Ray of her step-father's death. Schirrmann's widow understood that the personal and symbolic bridge that these two men had formed was important. She asked Ms. Barse to give Ray the name and address of another man who was part of the crew of the *U-862*. The man was Anton Kretschmann, a mechanic on the *U-862*, and at age 72, the youngest surviving member of the crew.

Kretschmann and Laenen began to correspond almost immediately. Like Albert Schirrmann, Anton Kretschmann remained in contact with the remaining members of his U-boat crew, and faithfully attended the annual reunions. In one of his first letters to Ray, Anton Kretschmann made an amazing gesture of reconciliation – he invited Ray and Norma Laenen to attend the next reunion of the *U-862* crew.

The Laenens were unable to attend that year because of a schedule conflict. Another invitation was extended the following year, but again, the Laenens could not make it. In 2000, the schedule was clear, and Ray and Norma Laenen, at last, made arrangements to visit Germany and meet U-boat machinist Anton Kretschmann. Alas, it was to be a personal visit, and not at a meeting of the *U-862* crew.

That year, Anton and Magdalene Kretschmann had celebrated their fiftieth wedding anniversary with a trip to Budapest, Hungary, and for the first time were unable to attend the *U-862* reunion. For that reason, the meeting would take place at Kretschmann's home, and not at the larger reunion of the *U-862* survivors.

In retrospect, Ray believes that this was probably for the better. While he was excited to meet his former enemy in person, he doesn't know if it would have been the same to be the *only* survivor of the *SS Peter Silvester* - at a reunion of the men who were instrumental in the sinking of that ship.

In June of 2000, Ray and Norma Laenen flew to Europe on an extraordinary mission of friendship and forgiveness. They stopped first in Belgium to visit relatives. After spending a few days with loved ones, they headed out in a rental car, and drove from Antwerp, Belgium to Gummersbach, Germany. On the road leading from Antwerp, Ray could look down from the highway, and see the town of Oevel – including the house in which he was born. How ironic it was that Ray Laenen, American citizen, traveled thousands of miles from his home in St. Clair Shores, Michigan to visit a German man who, some fifty-five years earlier had been his sworn enemy. A man who, in merely doing his job, had helped to sink the *SS Peter*

Silvester Liberty Ship, killing Chuck Briley and thirty-one other Allied soldiers. And yet, Anton Kretschmann lived no more than 150 miles from the town where Ray Laenen was born.

The Laenens motored across the Autobahn through the German cities of Aachen and Köln (Cologne) toward the city of Gummersbach. As the couple neared their destination, Ray said to Norma, "Honey, do you realize what we are doing here? We are going to visit a man who was a participant in the sinking of my ship! Thirty-two men were killed, and here we are, going to visit that man."

The significance of the moment was not lost on Norma. In yet one more of those strange little coincidences, the Gummersbach hotel in which the Laenens would sleep that night was called the "*Victors.*" At the time, Ray saw a coincidental connection to the University of Michigan fight song, *Hail to the Victors*, not realizing an even larger irony – that of an American victor visiting the home of a defeated German soldier.

With nervous anticipation, Ray Laenen rang the doorbell at the home of Anton Kretschmann. A man and woman came to the door, and Ray said "Anton? Magdalene?"

"Ray? Norma?" was the reply. The couples hugged each other and Anton invited the American visitors into his home. Although neither Anton nor Magdalene spoke any English, their son Gart was on hand to interpret in passable English. Ray and Norma were able to make out a few words that were similar to Flemish. A bottle of wine helped to ease the small talk, and the ice was quickly broken. Anton took Ray into his den and showed him his collection of military ship models and wall of photographs. He showed Ray one of his favorite models, a hand built replica of the *U-862*. A framed photo of *Korvettenkapitan* Heinrich Timm, the commander of the *U-862*, held a central place of honor in the gallery.

Norma and Ray share a glass of wine with the Kretschmanns

Anton informed Ray that he had invited another guest to join them. It was Günter Nethge, who had served alongside Anton Kretschmann as a radio operator on the *U-862*. After the war, Nethge had spent more than a year in a British POW camp in Wales (several of the *U-862* crewmembers still live in the U.K, having stayed on after the war).

When he later returned to his home in East Germany along the Russian border, Nethge wanted no part of the communist bloc country his homeland had become. He moved first to Frankfort in East Germany, and later to Buenos Aires, Argentina, where he built a successful import/export business. He was now retired and living once again in Frankfort. When Günter arrived at the Kretschmann home, Ray noticed that his Mercedes Benz bore a distinctive personalized license plate that simply read: "U-862."

Gunter Nethge's license plate

All parties at the home of Anton Kretschmann remained cordial, if not friendly. The perspective of fifty-some years had allowed this disparate group of men to come together in a spirit of rapprochement. They shared glasses of wine and stories of their experiences almost as if they had served together on the same boat. A tragic moment had brought each of them to the same place at the same time more than fifty years ago. Now they were together again, only this time by choice and with a high degree of empathy and mutual understanding.

L to R: Anton Kretschmann, Ray Laenen and Gunter Nethge

At one point in the evening Gart Kretschmann took Ray aside and thanked him for coming to visit his father.

"You don't know," he said, "how much this means to my father. After all you went through, you came all the way from the United States to visit my father. I can't thank you enough."

With that sentiment, tears fell from the eyes of both men. While some on both sides of the war have long since forgiven their former antagonists, it was a special honor for these men, to do so in person.

Anton and Ray in front of Anton's wall of souvenirs

Anton and Ray with model of U-862 in foreground

To this day, Ray Laenen and Anton Kretschmann continue to maintain periodic correspondence. While the event of these two old soldiers meeting face to face for the first time was poignant, it was not the only significant meeting that Ray would have. There was another major surprise that had occurred a year earlier back in Michigan.

One day in the early winter of 1998, Ray and Norma attended a Christmas raffle and dinner for St. Gertrude's Parish at the Barton House hall in St. Clair Shores. While there, Ray spotted Cliff Maison, an old friend and fellow parishioner at St. Gertrude Church. Ray walked over to Cliff's table and teased him about a photo in the recent Goodfellows Newspaper, which featured a photo of Cliff with the 1939 St. Gertrude High School basketball team. Ray teased Cliff about his old-fashioned basketball shorts and skinny legs.

Ray knew Cliff, but did not really know Cliff's wife, who was also seated at that table. Ray decided to walk Mr. and Mrs. Maison back to his own table to greet Norma and some other friends. As they walked toward the table, Cliff's wife took hold of Ray's arm and said that there was something she had wanted to ask him for a long time. As it turns out, she had read the 1980 *Detroit Free Press* story about the friendship and wartime experiences of Ray and Tom Tschirhart.

"As it happens," said Mrs. Maison, "I had a boyfriend during the war, in fact we were engaged, but he was killed when a German U-boat torpedoed his ship – in the Indian Ocean." Ray looked up at the woman with a puzzled expression. Something was beginning to click. A flicker of recognition. The woman continued.

"His name was Chuck..."

Before the words came out of her mouth, Ray finished her sentence.

"...Briley," they both said in unison. A chill ran down Ray's spine.

"You're Marie!" he cried.

"Yes, of course I am," said Marie Maison.

She was surprised that Ray had not remembered her name. With that introduction, Ray sat Marie down and described in detail the last moments of her former fiancé's life. He told her how often Chuck Briley had spoken of her and how much he had loved her. More than fifty years after she lost her fiancé halfway around the world, a chance encounter at a church dinner had provided the closure she never had. Such ghosts from the past can be quite unsettling. It was a bit awkward, for after all, Marie had been happily married to Cliff Maison for more than fifty years. Still, the persistence of memory would occasionally allow her a thought of her old beau. Ray Laenen was, once again, in awe of the wondrous connectedness of life.

The twenty first century would bring more surprises, and yet more closure for Ray Laenen. He continued to speak to children and veterans' groups about his war experience. As he did, he began to see that his words were hitting their mark. Children appeared to understand the sacrifices that were made by Ray and people like him in the Second World War. One young man brought Ray to tears when, in the course of introducing him as the speaker, the boy echoed one of Ray's favorite phrases – "Freedom is not Free."

It was clear that Ray's story needed to be told – and retold. David Stevens had mentioned Ray Laenen and Tom Tschirhart when he finally published his book *U-Boat Far from Home* in 1997. Stevens even used a part of Ray's letter to Albert Schirrmann as the opening of his epilogue.

In the summer of 2002, Ray was asked to participate in a live telephone interview as part of Martin Hewittson's *Hindsight* program on Australian radio. The Australian Broadcast Company arranged for a live feed from Michigan State University in Lansing, where Ray contributed his part of the conversation. Several Australians, including David Stevens, participated at the other end. It seemed that the story of Ray Laenen's wartime adventures was beginning to take on a life of its own.

At about the same time, Ray became aware of the Veteran's History Project. In October 2000, The United States Congress had authorized funds for the creation of a project with the goal of honoring United States War Veterans. The idea was to collect the personal war stories of those who served from WWI to the Persian Gulf Wars. By participating in this project, Ray realized, he could have his story immortalized in the Library of Congress. He jumped at the chance, and in 2001, told his story one more time for posterity. It was video recorded at Grosse Pointe South High School, and sent to Washington, D.C., to forever be a part of our national heritage.

Two years later, in the summer of 2003, Ray recorded a second telling of the same story, this time at the Macomb County Retired Seniors Volunteer Program in Clinton Township. That version was also sent to the Veteran's History Project in Washington. With these two videos now a permanent part of our National records, Ray Laenen's story will forever remain a part of the history of this country. This is the strand that was added to the fabric of America on that day in 1927 when Remie Laenen passed through Ellis Island.

Sixty years ago, Ray Laenen and many Americans like him – male, female, black, white, Christian and Jew, defended our freedoms from tyrants who spread terror throughout the world. On September 11, 2001, Ray was reminded once more that freedom is not free. Coming out of daily mass at St. Gertrude Church that morning, Ray started his car and, like always, heard the radio come to life. He recalls that on that clear and sunny morning, he had parked his car next to a dumpster so as to minimize the likelihood of receiving a door ding.

As he listened to the somber tone of the broadcast, he knew that something bad had happened in New York City. Just as had happened on that morning in December of 1941, he did not immediately know the extent of the damage or the gravity of the moment. When he arrived at home, he switched on the television to learn with the rest of America that for only the second time in his lifetime, our country had been attacked on our own soil. Once again, an enemy who acted out of a perverted notion of religious or ethnic purity had attacked us without warning. Soon, Ray knew all to well, Americans would once again have to go to battle in defense of our liberty. While the faces of our enemies may change, the cost of freedom remains the same.

In the 1980s, Chrysler Chairman Lee Iacocca initiated a drive to honor the immigrants who had come through Ellis Island, by restoring the landmark and offering plaques which could be purchased to honor loved ones. Ray and Norma Laenen each bought plaques to honor their parents.

In March of 2004, Ray and Norma went on a cruise to Alaska with their daughter Carrie and her husband Denny. While on the cruise, they met a soldier from Utah who was vacationing with his wife while on furlough from the war in Iraq. Ray naturally struck up a conversation with this man and thanked him sincerely for his service to our country. The man mentioned that he was disillusioned to come back and see all of the negative coverage of the war by our national media. He told Ray that our forces were accomplishing a great deal of good in that part of the world, but that the television and newspapers only seemed to be interested in showing the anger, hatred and destruction. Ray gave the man his address and phone number, and sincerely invited him to stay with the Laenens the next time they came anywhere near Detroit.

Pacific Theater section of WWII Memorial

Almost sixty years after the sinking of the *SS Peter Silvester,* our nation finally paid tribute to the men and women who had sacrificed so much to preserve our freedom in World War II. On May 29, 2004, Ray and Norma Laenen sat with 150,000 other Americans who attended the dedication ceremonies for the National World War II Memorial in Washington D.C. The fact that it took us so long to formally recognize what was perhaps the most amazing accomplishment of the twentieth century speaks volumes about the humility of that generation of Americans. We didn't do it sooner because they never asked us to. They never asked for our thanks. They did what they had to do and then got on with their lives. In so doing, they gave us a model for future generations. We can only hope, of course, to follow their lead and to learn from Ray Laenen and others like him what they already learned themselves: that freedom is never free.

Epilogue

Ray and Norma Laenen still live in the fine stone house on Jefferson Avenue in St. Clair Shores. It is the only home they have lived in during their fifty-six year marriage. The castle-like house stands in testament to the rock solid values of the Laenens and others of their generation. After all of these years together, Ray remains smitten, and Norma enamored of the man she married.

All five of the Laenen children live in Michigan, the farthest within a three-hour car ride of home. Ray and Norma now have eleven grandchildren, four great grandchildren, and a dog named Liberty - Libby for short.

Gary, the oldest, lives in Harbor Springs with his wife Carol and son David. He is retired from a career in commercial real estate, and his wife is retired from her job at Ameritech. Gary's two sons from a prior marriage both attend Wayne State University in Detroit.

Rick and his wife Diane live in St. Clair, Michigan just up the river from St. Clair Shores. They have two children, Rick Jr. and Kelli. Rick Jr. has two children of his own. Rick the senior works as a sales manager for Allied Building Products.

Norma and Ray – still smitten after all these years

Bob, a gentle and articulate man, lives in the family home and has responsibility for maintaining the investment properties owned by his parents. He is a good amateur musician and an avid iceboat racer.

Carrie lives in Lapeer with her husband Denny Pleva, their daughter Melissa and one grandchild. They have two other adult children.

Kim, the youngest of the Laenen children lives the closest to home in Chesterfield, Michigan, about ten miles north of St. Clair Shores. They have three children. Kim owns Acoustical Distributors, Inc., a company that provides acoustical ceiling tiles and similar products. Being the closest to home, Kim and his family come for breakfast with his parents every Sunday morning.

Tom Morawski died in 1988 but his wife Aggie still lives in Eastpointe, about five miles from the Laenens.

Tom Spicketts lives with his wife Virginia in Kalamazoo, and visits Ray three or four times per year. When they can't get together in person, they send each other birthday and Christmas cards.

Norma serves birthday cake to Tom Spicketts

Tom Tschirhart is retired from a career in sales. He lives with his wife Dorothy in Lady Lake, Florida for most of the year, but they return to Michigan each summer. He and Ray have been friends now for more than sixty-five years - and counting.

Ray and Tom Tschirhart today

Bob Taylor, the sailor from the HMS Activity, has maintained his correspondence with Ray Laenen. The two men are planning to meet each other for the first time in September 2005 when Taylor and his wife visit Detroit.

Recent photo of Bob and Jean Taylor

Don Tuthill and Chuck Kemmer also live in Michigan and see Ray occasionally.

Chuck Kemmer, Don Tuthill, Ray Laenen, and their wives

There is a granite monument at Southeastern High School in Detroit, bearing the name of Chuck Briley and others who died in the war. The St. Rose church and school have long since been torn down, but the old social hall remains, now serving the function of a charter school for inner city children.

Ray still exchanges Christmas cards and occasional letters with Anton Kretschmann and Gunter Nethge.

The broken hull of the *SS Peter Silvester* rests somewhere at the bottom of the Indian Ocean. The *U-862* passed into Japanese hands following the defeat of the Germans and was recovered by the British after the war. Since it was no longer needed by either side, the *U-862* was towed out of Singapore Harbor into the Straits of Malacca on February 15, 1946, and sunk by a British anti-submarine vessel.

Of the 2710 Liberty Ships built during World War II, only two remain to this day: the *SS Robert H. Brown* and the *SS Jeremiah O'Brien*. The *Robert H Brown* is docked in Baltimore Harbor and the *Jeremiah O'Brien* in San Francisco. Both ships are open to the public for tours.

The SS Jeremiah O'Brien Liberty Ship photographed in San Francisco

Bibliography for *Liberty Ship Survivor*

Ambrose, S. *The Good Fight: How World War II was Won*, Atheneum Books for Young Readers, New York, 2001

Anders, L. *The Ledo Road: General Joseph W. Stillwell's Highway to China*, University of Oklahoma Press, Norman, 1965

Black, W. C. Lt. (jg) (D) –L, *S. S. Peter Silvester: Report of Action with the Enemy*, U.S. Navy Classified Document, 1945, Declassified 1954

Brokaw, T. *The Greatest Generation*, Random House, New York, 2004

Burgan, M. *Belgium: Enchantment of the World*, Children's Press, New York, 2000

Clark, J. H., Pvt., *Tin Fish and Free Cigarettes*, Unpublished monograph, 1945, by permission of the author.

Elphick, P. *Liberty: The Ships that Won the War*, Naval Institute Press, Annapolis, 2001

Hewittson, M., (host) *Hindsight*, Australian Broadcasting Company, date unknown

Laabs, K. *MARS Task Force: 612th Field Artillery Battalion (PK), Attached to the 5332nd Brigade (Prov.)* Unpublished monograph, by permission of the author.

Loder, D. *The Land and People of Belgium*, J.B. Lippincott, Philadelphia, 1973

Moser, D., Editor, *China Burma India: World War II*, Time-Life Books, Alexandria, 1978

Stevens, D. *U-Boat far from Home: The Epic Voyage of U-862 to Australia and New Zealand*, Allen & Unwin, Sydney, 1997

Sulzberger, C.L., *The American Heritage Picture History of World War II*, American Heritage Publishing Co., 1966

U.S. Maritime Service Veterans, *Website* @ USMM.org

Verthe, A., *150 Years of Flemings in Detroit*, Lanoo/Tielt, Brussels, 1983

Index

Churchill, Winston 53, 55
Clark, Pvt. Jim 77
Clary Multiplier 146
Colombo, Ceylon (Sri Lanka)
  41, 69, 71
Corregidor 121
Cummins Diesel 148, 150

D

D-Day 40, 67
Daelemans, Josephine 5, 6, 9,
  10, 11, 12, 13, 17, 20, 109, 110,
  137, 140, 141, 153, 155
Daelemans family 5
Damman, Adolph 8
Damman, James 8
DeCoster, Peter 7
Dee's Bar 145
DeMeulemeester, Norma 20,
  137, 141
DeMeulemeester family 21, 25,
  137, 155
Dennis, Captain Bernard 68,
  78, 79, 86, 87
Detroit xi, 5, 7, 8, 9, 10, 12, 15,
  16, 18, 20, 21, 23, 24, 27, 36,
  37, 38, 108, 112, 126, 136, 137,
  139, 145, 147, 148, 150, 151,
  154, 164, 165, 175, 179, 181,
  184, 186
Detroit Business University
  (DBU) 139
Detroit Free Press 18, 150, 165,
  175

Diehl, Neal 163
Doolittle, Colonel James 119

E

Easley, Second Mate Jack 87,
  88, 90, 96
Eisenhower, General Dwight D.
  129, 130
Ellis Island 7, 9, 33, 177, 178
Enigma code 71

F

Flemish, people, language, art
  2, 5, 7, 13, 16, 170
Flying Tigers, The 45
Fort Ord, California 40
Fort Riley, Kansas 32, 33, 37,
  40, 163
Fort Sheridan, Illinois 31, 32
Francisco, Mrs. 128
Francisco, Pacita (Pacy) 127,
  128, 134

G

Garland Manufacturing 150,
  151
Gilbert's Bar 20
Gilbert family 20
Gladwin Street 9, 10, 11
Greenbrier Hotel (Ashford
  General Hospital) 125
Grosse Pointe, Michigan 7, 21,
  141, 161, 177

Gummersbach, Germany 165, 169, 170

H

Hannick, Father Emmett, Ph.D. 27

Hartlieb, Kurt 150, 151, 152

Hartlieb Steel Inc. 151, 152

Hatfield, Captain Charles 87, 96, 98, 99, 100

Herentals, town of 5

Hewittson, Martin 82, 176

Hillger Street 17, 137

Hisashi, Rear Admiral Mito 83

HMS Activity 98, 99, 100, 101, 102, 103, 104, 158, 184

Hollywood Hospital 104, 105, 109, 111

Hoover, Russ 164

House, Clinton 158

hump, the 46

I

Iacocca, Lee 178

Immaculate Heart of Mary (IHM), Sisters of the xi, 17, 18, 19, 23, 25, 163

immersion foot 96, 105, 125

Indian Ocean x, 2, 67, 71, 72, 73, 85, 90, 95, 112, 125, 153, 161, 175, 186

Iraq, war in 25, 178

J

Jones, Hope (Esperanza) 127

K

Kaiser, Henry J. 58, 60, 77

Kaisersarg (Kaiser coffin) 77

Kemmer, Chuck xi, 40, 41, 77, 80, 87, 88, 92, 113, 121, 160, 185

Kleckner, Stan 155

Kretschmann, Anton 168, 169, 170, 171, 172, 173, 174, 175, 186

L

Laabs, Ken xi, 43, 51, 52, 64

Laenen, (Ray) Remie 2, 6, 9, 10, 13, 16, 17, 18, 19, 20, 21, 22, 23, 24, 25, 33, 37, 110, 130, 135, 141, 177

Laenen, Bob v, 147

Laenen, Carrie v

Laenen, Gary v, 146, 147, 153, 181

Laenen, Gustaf 2, 3, 4, 5, 6, 7, 8, 9, 10, 11, 12, 17, 20, 22, 24, 25, 108, 110, 137, 140, 141, 153, 155

Laenen, Joe 147

Laenen, Josephine 5, 6, 8, 9, 10, 11, 12, 13, 17, 20, 108, 109, 110, 137, 140, 141, 153, 155

M

About the Author

Joe N. Mazzara is a Detroit Area Psychologist and freelance writer. In addition to *LIBERTY SHIP SURVIVOR*, he is also the author of the memoir, *Pedal Cars and Purple Pickles* (AuthorHouse, 2001). He has published articles in several magazines and newspapers, including *Acoustic Guitar Magazine, The Open Exhaust* and *The Michigan Catholic.* In his free time, he writes yet-to-be-published fiction, as well as an ongoing column called *From the Back Pew* for his local church paper, the St. Valerie of Ravenna *Valerian.* He currently teaches Psychology at Macomb Community College in his hometown of Clinton Township, Michigan. He and his wife Cindy have two children, Mark and Kate.

Printed in the United States
35847LVS00003B/274-291